THE COLLECTOR'S CHOPIN
AND SCHUMANN

THE COLLECTOR'S

Chopin

AND

Schumann

Harold C. Schonberg

J. B. LIPPINCOTT COMPANY

Philadelphia & New York

First Edition

Printed in the United States of America

Library of Congress Catalog Card Number
59-6434

The listings in this volume are considerably revised and updated versions of discographies that
were written for *High Fidelity* magazine. I am
grateful to Mr. Charles Fowler, publisher of *High
Fidelity*, for permission to use the material here.
Sections of the essays on Chopin and Schumann
originally appeared in the *Musical Courier* and are
reprinted here with the kind permission of Gid
Waldrop, editor of that publication.

H. C. S.

To My Parents

Contents

THE COLLECTOR'S CHOPIN
AND SCHUMANN

CHOPIN, SCHUMANN AND
THE ROMANTIC AGE

First, in 1803, came Berlioz. Then, within the
space of ten years, came the other great early
romantics—Mendelssohn in 1809; Schumann and
Chopin in 1810; Liszt in 1811; Wagner in 1813.
Verdi was also born in 1813; he is not normally
considered one of the romantics and is something of a special case. With the exception of
Verdi, all of these composers were in touch with
one another during various phases of their creative careers. It was Schumann who introduced
Chopin to Europe with his celebrated review
("Hats off, gentlemen, a genius!") in an 1831
issue of the *Allegmeine musikalische Zeitung.*
Chopin and Liszt played piano four hands at
Parisian soirées, and Liszt was to write the first
biography of Chopin. Berlioz and Mendelssohn
met and struck up an uneasy friendship (in a
letter to his parents from Italy, Mendelssohn
described his new friend as "a stereotyped genius
in black and white"), exchanging batons and
causing a flurry of Cooperesque prose from
Berlioz ("Great chief! We have promised to

11

exchange tomahawks. Here is mine, which is
rough; yours is too plain. . . ."). Schumann and
Mendelssohn were extremely close friends; indeed, everybody was a friend to the rich, cultured, phenomenally gifted Mendelssohn. Liszt
was naturally among that number, and he was
also one of the first to take up the cause of that
late starter, Richard Wagner. Wagner argued
music and politics with Schumann in Dresden.
Schumann reviewed the Berlioz *Symphonie fantastique*—a model of what a piece of music
criticism should be. Of all these, Chopin was the
most withdrawn. He apparently took little interest in the contemporary romantic upheaval
around him; could not understand or respond
to the paintings of his good friend Delacroix;
showed no reaction to the music of Berlioz or
Schumann; was not particularly well-read. Yet
he was one of the revolutionary forces of nine-
teenth-century music.

But all of these romantic composers were
revolutionary—Schumann perhaps most of all,
Mendelssohn least of all. Romantic, romanticism:
fine, sonorous words capable of no exact meaning. Bach and Mozart are supposed to be "classic"
composers. Yet Bach could write the *Chromatic
Fantasy*, which Huneker called "white-hot with
passion" and a thoroughly "romantic" efful-
gence; and Mozart could write the introduction
to the C major Quartet, with its strange dis-

sonances unmatched in music until the present century. As Jacques Barzun has pointed out in his study of Berlioz: "Scholars who find Romanticist germs in seventeenth-century Pietism, or in eighteenth-century sentimentality and nature worship, are perfectly correct. For the neoclassicism of those centuries had its dissenters, who grew more numerous as time went on, and from them the Romanticists properly so-called drew important elements."

All one can do, trying to define romanticism, is speak in generalities. The French Revolution and the Industrial Revolution brought new concepts of liberty to the world—political liberty and physical liberty. For with the development of the steam engine, people, and hence ideas, could move much faster. Mankind suddenly developed a sense of the importance of the individual. The Church and the aristocracy no longer had its previous iron control over the people, and the middle class began to assert itself. Around the turn of the century, Wordsworth, Byron and the other English romantic poets had brought new concepts to poetry—concepts which quickly percolated to the other arts. Away with classicism! Away with long, stuffy, "correct" writing! Individuality above everything! Rousseau had previously stated it: "I am different from all other men I have seen. If I am not better, at least I am different."

And thus was spawned the world of the romantics—dream, vision, the concept of art for art's sake as opposed to the craftsmanship and artisanship of the previous generations of creators. Bach, Haydn and Mozart were never sentimental, but all of the romantics could be, often embarrassingly so. Bach probably would have laughed had he been called an artist. Schumann and Liszt would have been mightily insulted had they *not* been called so. They, and their fellow composers, took their work and their contributions to posterity very seriously: especially their contributions to posterity. But Bach, one feels sure, was scarcely interested in posterity. He was too busy, for one thing. He had to turn out a cantata a week, student pieces, commissions; teach, play the organ, run a school; and he knew that when he was gone, his successor at the *Thomas-Kirche* would bundle up the Bach MSS and start turning out *his* cantatas and student pieces and other assignments.

Unlike the earlier composers, the romantics, most of them, were not exclusively devoted to writing music. A good number of them wrote professionally *about* it. The two finest critics of the day, and perhaps of any day, were Berlioz and Schumann. Liszt contributed some weighty pieces of journalism, and the collected prose of Richard Wagner fills volume after volume. For almost the first time in history, too, is found the phenomenon of the composer making his own way in the world without patronage of any kind. Even the independent and explosive Handel had had dukes and kings helping him along. Bach was taken care of by Church authorities. Haydn had his Eszterházy; Mozart his Archbishop of Salzburg (and, after his break with the Archbishop, poor Mozart spent the rest of his short life unsuccessfully looking for a patron and died in poverty; the times were not ripe for him). Beethoven had his Lichnowskys, Lobkowitzs and Kinskys. The romantics had nobody. Chopin made his living by being the most sought-after society teacher of piano in Paris. Berlioz was a music critic and conductor. Schumann taught, in addition to his journalistic chores. Liszt made a fortune playing the piano. Mendelssohn, of course, was independently wealthy. He busied himself with educational activities and was instrumental in founding the Leipzig Conservatory of Music in 1843 (for which Schumann was named professor of composition). And, in addition, each of the romantics realized a certain steady income from the sale of their music. This was something almost unheard of in musical economics (Beethoven, however, had led the way).

Chopin, the Pole who settled in Paris, and Schumann, the German who seldom left his own

country, were born the same year and came into
flower at about the same time. Both brought
something new to music; and, with the exception
of Berlioz, they are the most important of the
early romantics. For Mendelssohn, gifted as he
was (his Octet for Strings, composed when he
was sixteen, stands unprecedented in the history
of music, and not even Mozart could boast of
such an achievement at such an age), lacked the
imagination to carry out his early promise, while
Liszt and Wagner turned out their major works
long after the earlier trinity had accomplished
theirs. Schumann, the ardent and very consciously romantic composer, could well be the
most individual, intensely personal musician who
ever lived. He broke all the rules, as they were
then understood, evolved his own theories based
less on precedent than any composer who ever
lived, never consciously wrote a cheap note, and
spent a life in sheer dedication to music. Chopin,
who concentrated on the piano (as did Schumann up to his Op. 24), was never consciously
the romantic that Schumann was; at least, he
made no great protestations and did not rush to
the esthetic barricades waving a flag. Nor was
his personality as sweet, sympathetic and noble
as Schumann's. But he, too, was a flaming genius
who revolutionized the nature of writing for the
piano; whose harmonic ingenuity was such that
it left its mark on the entire century—and this

despite the fact that he worked mostly in small forms. But smallness does not necessarily equate with esthetic worth. It was George Sand who said that there was more music in the thirteen measures of Chopin's C minor Prelude than in the four-hour trumpetings of a Meyerbeer opera. Sand was biased, but she was right.

Chopin and Schumann may have been light-years apart temperamentally, but they stood for much the same things in music. Toward the end of Schumann's life he encountered the young Brahms and was so impressed that he wrote an enthusiastic article about the young genius. He called the article "New Paths." But Schumann was, in a way, wrong. It was not Brahms who was destined to strike off on new paths. That already had been done, in the Eighteen-Thirties, by Schumann himself and by his great Polish contemporary.

Frédéric François Chopin

Born Zelazowa Wola, Poland, February 22, 1810;
died Paris, October 17, 1849

In the early Eighteen-Thirties, who were the
"great" composers? Schumann, in the introduction to his critical writings, mentions some. "The
musical situation was not then very encouraging
in Germany," he noted. "On the stage Rossini
reigned, at the pianoforte nothing was heard but
Herz and Hünten; and yet but a few years had
passed since Beethoven, Weber and Schubert
lived among us. It is true that Mendelssohn's star
was ascending, and wonderful things were re-
lated of Chopin. . . ." These words were aimed
at the decade from 1825 to 1835, and Schumann
could have added a great many more names.
There were Hummel and Spohr, Moscheles,
Kalkbrenner, Gyrowetz—all important, highly
respected men in their day, all virtually forgotten
today. It was the day of the virtuoso-composer;
the day of potpourris and Grand Operatic Fan-
tasias on this and that.

19

By all rights, Chopin should have ended up *à la* Kalkbrenner and Henri Herz. Chopin too was a virtuoso-composer who started his career writing flashy pieces and operatic transcriptions. But one thing saved him. He had genius and the others didn't. And what genius! The Warsaw in which Chopin spent his childhood was not one of the major cultural centers of Europe. Chopin grew up having taught himself more than his teachers ever taught him. He had not been greatly exposed to the new ideas that were sweeping the Continent. Yet at the age of twenty, when he left Poland for good, his style was to all intents and purposes fully formed. Already he had composed some of the études, the F minor Piano Concerto, several mazurkas, polonaises and other works. He was what the botanists call a "sport"—an inexplicable flowering that neither heredity nor environment can account for.

Heredity consisted of a father, Nicholas Chopin, who was French-born and had emigrated to Poland in 1787, and a mother of humble birth who had been born in Poland. Her name was Tekla Yustina Kzhizhanovska. They had four children, of whom Frédéric was the second (there were Ludvika, born in 1807; Sabela, born in 1811, and Emilya, born in 1813). As far as environment goes, the Chopin household was a normally musical one for those days. Father played the flute and violin; mother sang and played the piano. No financial problems seem to have bothered the Chopins, who brought up their children in good middleclass circumstances. Ludvika learned to play the piano, as all good children do, and apparently she had talent. But soon it was discovered that tiny Frédéric cried bitterly when sounds displeased him, laughed when they were pleasant. When Frédéric was six years old, he pleaded for piano lessons, and he and Ludvika commenced studies under a teacher named Adalbert Zhivny. Frédéric made giant strides, and started composing. His first composition was a G minor Polonaise—he was about seven years old at the time. He made his debut as a pianist at the age of eight, playing a piano concerto by Adalbert Gyrowetz, one of the fashionable pianist-composers of the time. The result was a fabulous success, and young Chopin was made much of by the Polish aristocracy, hailed as a new Mozart and in general petted and spoiled. Fortunately none of this seems to have gone to his head. In most respects his boyhood was quite normal— apart, of course, from his musical genius.

Most of Chopin's formal musical training came from Joseph Elsner, the director of the Warsaw Conservatory. Elsner soon found out the type of boy he had on his hands, and he was ready to admit that young Chopin knew more than he did. At Chopin's final examinations, Elsner noted:

"amazing capabilities; musical genius." All Warsaw was proud of its *Wunderkind*, and friends saw to it that he had opportunities to seek his fortune in more cosmopolitan cities. Chopin made a trip to Berlin, appeared in Vienna as a pianist-composer (he was well received but reported that there were some complaints about the delicacy of his playing), toured Germany and finally settled for good in Paris.

During his fledgling trips he was constantly writing home. He was intelligent, observant, and his letters are lively, witty and sometimes malicious. He could have developed into an admirable, pithy prose stylist, and it is our loss that he never, as so many of the romantics did, turned to criticism. One point of interest in his letters is the love he reveals for the singing voice: strange, for he composed only one set of vocal pieces, the Seventeen Polish Songs. But it is easy to see where the cantilena of the singing voice, especially in the operas of his beloved Bellini, influences his own melodic style. Time and time again Chopin writes of the operas and singers he admired: *Der Freischütz*, Henrietta Sontag, Pasta, Rubini, Malibran, Nourrit, Rossini's *Otello* and *Siege of Corinth*, Meyerbeer's *Robert le Diable*. He seldom comments on other composers' music, though when he heard Beethoven's last string quartet he was moved to a wonderful bit of capsule criticism: "I haven't heard anything so great for a long time. Beethoven snaps his fingers at the whole world."

It was as a pianist-composer that Chopin arrived in Paris in 1831. What a time to be there! Victor Hugo, Sainte-Beuve, Balzac, Gautier, Mérimée, de Vigny, de Musset, Heine, Guizot, Stendhal, Lamartine, Sue, Dumas *père*, Delacroix, Ingres, Corot, Berlioz, Auber, Adam, Hérold, Liszt, Rossini, Bellini, Meyerbeer, Cherubini—a galaxy! Young Chopin, who always had *savoir-faire* and plenty of confidence in himself, nevertheless could not have helped being dazzled by the intellectual climate that was then Paris. One proof of it is that this genius, one of the greatest and most individual pianists of all time, seriously considered taking piano lessons from the pedantic Friedrich Kalkbrenner, who gravely assured Chopin that three years of the *méthode Kalkbrenner* would *really* make something of him. Chopin for a while was swept off his feet. "You would not believe how curious I was about Herz, Liszt, Hiller, etc.," he wrote home. "They are all zero beside Kalkbrenner. . . . If Paganini is perfection, Kalkbrenner is his equal, but in quite another style." And more equally hysterical writing follows. Fortunately Chopin reconsidered, especially after a hasty and horrified reply from Elsner.

It was in his first days in Paris, too, that Chopin's attention was drawn to Schumann's glowing review of his Op. 2, the Variations on *Là ci darem la mano* from Mozart's *Don Giovanni*. Chopin was not only amused by the review; he even was ungrateful enough to poke fun at the author. "One can die of the imagination of this German," he concludes. Some years later they met; and whatever Chopin's private feelings, he kept them to himself. Anyway Clara Schumann, the composer's gifted wife, was playing Chopin's music in public—one of the first pianists to do so.

Chopin found Paris very much to his liking. He was immediately recognized as an unusual pianist and as a composer with something new to offer. But Chopin did not mix with musicians as much as he did with high society. He had perfect manners, dressed like a dandy, was something of a snob, and was, or professed to be, an anti-Semite (though that did not keep him from making friends with Jews provided they were wealthy). "I have got into the highest society," he wrote home. "I sit with ambassadors, princes, ministers. . . ." His students, of whom he never lacked during his life—and his fees were very high—were generally titled, or wealthy people in the highest class of society. (He had but one great pupil, a prodigy named Karl Filtsch who died at the age of fifteen. Liszt heard him and threw up his hands. "When he starts to make concert tours I shall shut up shop," he said.)

Chopin saved very little of the money he was making. "I have five lessons to give today," he once wrote. "You think I am making a fortune? Carriages and white gloves cost more, and without them one would not be in good taste." Good taste was extremely important to Chopin.

In the meantime, Chopin was composing steadily and, more important to him, was getting published steadily. He made money from his music and drove a very hard bargain with his publishers. A steady flow of mazurkas, waltzes and nocturnes came from his pen, in his delicate, precise, exquisite calligraphy. The greater works, too, were starting to come out—the scherzos, ballades, études, polonaises. It was during his early years in Paris, too, that signs of the tuberculosis, of which he was to die, made themselves felt. At best Chopin was never a robust man—or a robust pianist, for that matter. As his disease made inroads he found himself physically too weak to play a fortissimo on the piano. By 1840 he weighed no more than a hundred pounds. He envied Liszt his demonic power with an envy that only a weakling can feel for a strong man. During his life Chopin gave very few public recitals, because he knew that his tone was too small to fill a large hall, and he also knew that only connoisseurs were capable of appreciating what he was doing at the keyboard. Chopin did most of his playing in salons.

But while Chopin was physically weak, and a dandy to boot, there was nothing effeminate about him. As a boy he had his normal quota of love affairs, and the full story has yet to be written about his relations with his student countesses and princesses. Chopin could be very close-mouthed about his private affairs. Then, in 1836, he met Aurore Dudevant, the popular lady author who wrote under the name of George Sand. Soon they were living together. It was she who took him off to Majorca for what was supposed to be an idyllic summer: the Mediterranean breezes and the moon at night, he composing, she writing. This was the summer of 1838, and it turned out disastrously. Rain, poor food, few creature comforts, illness, a hemorrhage: Chopin returned to Paris barely alive.

Nevertheless the affair continued. If Chopin could have stood the sight of George Sand after Majorca, it is proof that he really was in love with her. They remained together until 1847. The story of their break-up has been variously told, depending on whose side the analyst was on. Sand had two children (not by Chopin), at least one of whom was legitimate. The son, Maurice, took a strong dislike to Chopin. The daughter, Solange, apparently a giddy girl, was fond of the composer. Maurice constantly worked to undermine Chopin's position. When Solange married the sculptor Auguste Jean-

Baptiste Clésinger, over the protests of her mother and brother, and when Chopin helped Solange, there was an explosion. When the smoke cleared away, Chopin and Sand were separated forever. She wrote a novel about the affair, in which Chopin, barely disguised, plays an unfavorable role.

Chopin had but two years to live. He gave his last public recital at the Salle Pleyel on February 16, 1848. Sick as he was, he dragged himself to England and Scotland at the behest of one of his pupils, Jane Stirling. Chopin at that time was in financial difficulties and he hoped to recoup. He did give some private concerts and took some pupils, but wrote complaining letters to friends about the state of his finances and the state of the Englishmen. In Scotland he was so bored he didn't know what to do. He had some tart comments to make about the people he saw. "Their orchestra is like their roast beef or their turtle soup; excellent, strong, but nothing more. . . . Every creature here seems to have a screw loose. . . . Those who know my compositions ask me: —'Jouez-moi votre second *Soupir*—j'aime beaucoup vos cloches.' And every observation ends with:—'Leik [*sic*] water,' meaning that it flows like water. I have not yet played to any Englishwoman without her saying to me:—'Leik water!!!' They all look at their hands and play the wrong notes with much feeling. Eccentric

folk, God help them." But it was the generous
Jane Stirling, who adored her little Chopin, who
sent him an anonymous gift of 25,000 francs that
helped make his last days easier. On his return to
Paris, Chopin was virtually helpless. "I am ready
to faint from fatigue and weariness," he wrote
the cellist Auguste Franchomme. On October
17 he died. His last words were scratched on a
sheet of paper. "As this earth will smother me,
I adjure you to have my body opened so that
I may not be buried alive."

As a composer he wrote almost exclusively for
the piano. Chopin had been born at exactly the
right time. The piano had been invented in 1709,
but not until the early years of the nineteenth
century had it been brought to the point where it
is substantially the same instrument that it is
today. Before then, the piano had little resonance,
nor did it have the lungs—the ability to sustain
tone or make a rich sound—that the modern
instrument has. Thus Mozart and even Beethoven
had to use a fairly close and rapid type of figuration, especially in the left hand. Carl Maria von
Weber and Johann Nepomuk Hummel, two of
the early piano virtuoso-composers, had done
much to extend the classical-derived type of
figuration, but not until Chopin came along were
the resources of the piano fully exploited. Chopin
completely freed the left hand. Where Mozart

would seldom write an accompaniment figure in excess of a fifth, Chopin delighted in long, rolling left-hand arpeggios that might cover several octaves. His études examine and broaden every aspect of piano technique, and no composer since then has been able to add very much to it (though men like Prokofieff in our own century began working on a different set of premises, taking the piano to be a percussive and not a cantabile instrument). Chopin also invented and brought to perfection a type of elaborate decoration (fioritura) functional to the melodic line. Where so many composers of his (and our) day will indulge in flashy but empty passagework, the mature Chopin, no matter how spectacular and glittering (as in the middle section of the F-sharp Impromptu), pinpoints each note so that it has meaning and expressivity. It is safe to say that there is a classical purity in Chopin's writing, in that the forms generally are a perfect, economical vehicle for the content.

His ear was infallible. Few composers have had equivalent skill in modulation. Chopin's harmonic innovations have been fully discussed in Gerald Abraham's *Chopin's Musical Style*, required reading for those interested in the composer. What has not been so thoroughly examined, though many authors have hinted at it, are the classical currents in Chopin. His favorite composers were, besides himself, Bach and Mozart, and of the two

it was Bach who excited him more. He probably
had the entire *Well-Tempered Clavier* by heart,
and he assigned the preludes and fugues of the
WTC as part of the regular fare of his students.
Chopin's twenty-four Preludes, like the *WTC*,
go through every major and minor key. Play the
very first Chopin Prelude, in C major, at a very
slow tempo, and follow it up with the C major
Prelude that opens Bach's *WTC*. You may have
the surprise of your life. There is even a sugges-
tion that Chopin may have originally conceived
the études as a neo-Bachian exercise. At least, the
key signatures of the first six have a definite
relationship: C major and A minor, E major and
C-sharp minor, G-flat major and E-flat minor
(the major and the relative minor). Then the
relationship straggles off, and Chopin apparently
gave up the idea. Once Chopin and Delacroix
had a visit, and Delacroix asked him what
constituted logic in music. Notes Delacroix,
in his *Journal*, "He made me feel what
counterpoint and harmony are; how the fugue
is like pure logic in music, and that to know the
fugue deeply is to be acquainted with the element of all reason and all consistency in music."
Chopin, the romanticist and one of the very first
of the nationalist composers (in his mazurkas and
polonaises), was instinctively a classicist. (Schumann, too, had a musical side strongly influenced
by Bach.)

Chopin lived to see himself established as a popular composer who had publishers running to him. Nor has his music lost its popularity. Many composers—Liszt, Mendelssohn—have had their ups and downs. Chopin's music, however, and nearly all of it, has been part of the permanent repertoire since his own lifetime. His music is very much with us and shows no signs of fading. At the same time, there is no doubt that a certain tradition of Chopin playing is disappearing. Our younger virtuosos, a hardy breed with steel fingers (and, one often suspects, souls), can spatter the notes of a Prokofieff concerto with the force and fluency of raindrops from an industrious tornado. When they come to a simple Chopin mazurka they seem nonplused. In a way their difficulty is understandable. It is hard to do precision work when wearing boxing gloves.

Now, the older school of romantic pianists, from Chopin himself to Artur Rubinstein and Guiomar Novaes of our own day, was as rugged a group of individualists as existed anywhere. There was Vladimir de Pachmann, with his exquisite traceries (and mannered eccentricity); and Anton Rubinstein, with his thunderous volleys of tone; and in between there was every conceivable kind of musical approach and philosophy.

But at least three things all these pianists had in common—a singing tone, a flowing legato and a natural rubato. Hofmann could rear up and smite the keyboard, sometimes actually with the flat of his hand. Yet he never lost tone. And he, like all the great pianists of the day, could take a phrase and connect its individual notes so that they flowed together in a melting, logical sequence. Fingers, pedal, brain and heart—all worked together.

The deficiency in legato playing of many of today's younger pianists strongly militates against their success as Chopinzees (so Huneker once described the species). Nor do they seem to be interested in experimenting with the tonal resources of the piano, its potentialities for color. Some of them seem afraid of the pedals, touching them gingerly as though a healthy charge of electricity were surging through them. One wonders how they practice. It was evident, when a great romantic pianist played Chopin, that he had spent hours on hours upon endless hours studying not only the notes but—much more important—what was beyond the notes. He experimented with inner voices (almost a lost art today), with accentuations, with varying finger weights, with contrasts of dynamics. It was all very personal; and yet what came out was always (well, nearly always) implicit in the music, free for all to discover.

Perhaps our present-day musical stringency is an inhibiting factor against the young pianist. He has been taught to respect the wishes of the composer. Well and good; but only too often that manifests itself in a cold, too-literal exposition of the notes. Accuracy is a wonderful thing; but let's make sure we are aiming at the right target. The only musical target worth shooting for is a re-creation, not a blueprint. Anyway, there never was a composer who did not expect the performer to add something of his own. What to add? That, of course, depends upon the taste of the performer, scholarship and an identification with a certain style. (Listen to Landowska's Bach for a concrete example.) Some have said that our younger pianists lack identification with the romantic school because they are children of a neurotic age and reflect that age. Perhaps there is some truth in the statement, though it does seem too easy and pat. Anything, these days, can be explained in psychiatric jargon. I myself put most of the blame on the teaching. Young recitalists, many of them from some of the most respected conservatories in the world, come before the public with appalling notions about music and an equally appalling lack of intellectual curiosity about it. They are proud because they can "play the notes." And how seldom does one come across a young pianist who communicates any real joy in making music!

It is also very rare that one hears a convincing rubato from a young pianist; and rubato is the

essence of Chopin. Much misleading nonsense
has been written about the term. Some years ago
this writer happened to be looking up something
or other in the 1910 edition of Grove and happened to light on "RUBATO, lit. 'robbed' or
'stolen'. . . ." It was a fairly short paragraph,
written by J. A. Fuller Maitland, and it described very well the idea of the term. But then
Fuller Maitland fell into an error prevalent at the
time. "This license," he wrote, "is allowable in
the works of all the romantic masters from
Weber downwards, with the single exception of
Mendelssohn, who had the greatest dislike to any
modification of the time that he had not specifically marked. In the case of the older masters,
it is entirely and unconditionally inadmissible,
and it may be doubted whether it should be
introduced in Beethoven. . . ."

That last sentence could not be more incor-
rect. Here is Mozart writing, in 1777: "What
these people cannot grasp is that in tempo rubato
in an Adagio, the left hand should go on playing
in strict time. With them, the left hand always
follows suit." And here is C. P. E. Bach, in his
The True Art of Playing Keyboard Instruments,
a book written around 1750. Bach is writing
about performance: attack, time values, accentuations and the like. "This brings us to the tempo
rubato," he says, and goes on to describe its
problems—how one hand must play against the
bar and the other with the bar (which Mozart

later echoed). "Proper execution of this tempo," continues C. P. E. Bach, "demands great critical faculties and a high order of sensibility. . . . However, practice alone will be of no help here, for without a fitting sensitivity, no amount of pains will succeed in contriving a correct rubato. As soon as the upper part begins slavishly to follow the bar, the essence of the rubato is lost, for then all the other parts must be played in time. *Most keyboard pieces contain rubato passages.*" (Italics added.)

So much for Fuller Maitland and his unfortunate lapse from scholarship. The amazing thing is that C. P. E. Bach and Mozart had pretty much the same conception of rubato that the romantics and moderns were to have. In the severe words of the *Harvard Dictionary of Music*, rubato is a term "that denotes a certain elasticity and flexibility of tempo consisting of slight accelerandos and ritardandos which alternate according to the requirements of the musical expression." Chopin said much the same thing: "The left hand is the conductor; it must not waver or lose ground; do with the right hand what you will and can." This statement was written down by Wilhelm von Lenz, who also quoted Chopin as saying: "Supposing that a piece lasts a given number of minutes; it may take just so long to perform the whole, but in the details deviations may occur." Liszt put it a little more flamboyantly in his well-known definition: "Do you see these trees? The wind plays in the leaves, life unfolds and develops beneath them, but the tree remains the same. That is the Chopin rubato." According to Jean Kleczynski, Liszt also described the Chopin rubato as "agitation," saying that "All the compositions of Chopin should be played observing the rules of accentuation and prosody, but with a certain agitation, the secret of which those who have never heard the master find it difficult to fathom."

It was Chopin who in his piano playing specialized in the rubato and gave it more prominence than it had ever had before. Under his fingers it was, in those days, a strange and even awesome phenomenon. Musicians of the older school had much trouble getting acclimated to it. Some never did.

Well known is the run-in Chopin had with Meyerbeer. It was described by von Lenz. It seems that von Lenz was taking a lesson with Chopin and was playing a mazurka when Meyerbeer strolled in. "That is two-four time," said Meyerbeer. Chopin beat out the rhythm, then counted it aloud. Meyerbeer still maintained that it was two-four. " 'It is *three*-four!' almost screamed Chopin, and played it himself. He played it several times, counted aloud, and stamped the time with his foot—he was beside himself! It was of no use. Meyerbeer insisted that it was two-four, and they parted in ill humor."

But Meyerbeer was not being pig-headed. Contemporary musicians simply found Chopin's beat hard to count. The young Charles Hallé, who was studying in Paris, had the opportunity to hear Chopin very often. In 1845 or 1846 he told Chopin that most of the mazurkas when played by Chopin himself appeared to be written not in three-four but in four-four time, "the result of his dwelling so much longer on the first note in the bar." This Chopin heatedly denied, whereupon Hallé "made him play one of them and counted audibly four in the bar, which fitted perfectly. Then he laughed and explained that it was the national character of the dance which created the oddity."

It worked the other way, too. When Chopin played a piece in four-four time, Hallé reported that there was a three-four feeling. Hallé, incidentally, took his life in his hands when he argued with Chopin about rhythms. It is surprising that he did not get his head bitten off. It was not until later that he learned about the quarrel between Chopin and Meyerbeer on that very subject. The Polish composer was always very touchy about his music and his pianism. Hallé sums up Chopin's playing with a comment about its most remarkable feature: "the entire freedom with which he treated the rhythm, but which appeared so natural that for years it had never struck me."

This is interesting. Under Chopin's magic

fingers, his "four-four" mazurkas undoubtedly sounded subtle and natural. But we need not take Hallé and Meyerbeer too literally. They probably were struck as from a thunderbolt by Chopin's rhythmic freedom and probably had difficulty rationalizing what they heard. The holds and displacements were to them so novel, one suspects, that they literally lost the power to count accurately. (Not a rare phenomenon, by the way; ask any conductor.) In any case, there can be no doubt that Chopin took considerable liberties with his own music.

No really evocative Chopin playing is possible without the most subtle of rubatos; and, unhappily, the current idea of rubato only too often involves actual distortion of note values instead of the delicate proportional relationships and adjustments that are the ideal. Harvey Grace once wrote an indignant piece in the *Musical Times*, protesting this "robbery with violence," and citing chapter and verse where certain pianists would make an eighth note out of a quarter, or a series of galloping couplets from a simple triplet figuration. Were he alive today he would *really* hear some hop-skip-jump piano playing in the name of rubato.

Thus rubato is a variation in tempo or rhythm that adds interest and tension to a melodic line without distorting it. It should not *ever* involve actual alteration of note values. Nor should it involve metrical shifts. The basic *meter* must always be maintained; it is the *rhythm* that may fluctuate. No composer, from Bach to Poulenc, would want his music played in a rigid, metronomic manner. He would want delicate shifts and adjustments, always expressed in proportional relationships. In a waltz, for example, the second beat may be held a trifle longer, but the idea of waltz meter should never be lost. Or you can bend a measure so that it takes off on a slightly different tangent from previous ones, but the individual notes in that measure continue to bear the same relationship to each other. An eighth note will remain an eighth note; a quarter note will remain a quarter note and not turn into a dotted quarter.

Old C. P. E. Bach was right. Rubato cannot be taught. It must be felt. A calculated rubato, one that proceeds from superimposed instruction rather than instinctive feeling, will be either eccentric or will develop into positive musical anarchy.

Next comes the consideration of technique; and technique is a *sine qua non* of Chopin playing. Name any great Chopin pianist and you name a great technician. For, after all, Chopin composed some of the most difficult music in the repertoire, and you can no more play it without technique to burn than you can tear down the Empire State Building with a toothpick. You may have the greatest musical instinct since Orpheus—but what good is it if you can't play the notes? If the point seems to be belabored here, it is because the cliché that "technique is merely a means to an end, not the end itself" is a half-truth that has done considerable harm. An instrumentalist cannot have too much technique. As a matter of fact, there are certain musical occasions where technique *is* an end in itself, but that is another story.

Of course there are additional prerequisites to great Chopin playing—poetry, color, flexibility, spontaneity, power, passion when needed. And passion is needed more often than not. For Chopin was no prissy, ultra-refined composer. Chopin was a seminal force. He borrowed from some composers—Hummel and John Field, to mention but two—but whatever he borrowed he made his own. Field, jealous of Chopin's success called him "a sickroom talent." Nothing could be less true. Although Chopin worked for the most part in small forms, he was a major musical thinker, and his best works are powerful and passionate. In addition, Chopin—more than Liszt, more than anybody else—*was* the piano. He himself was a paradox—a weak, tubercular man, precious, with a precise mind but a narrow frame of esthetic reference. Yet within him was a seething rebellion that often expressed itself in outbursts of explosive force and, willy-nilly, made him one of the great romantics. "Cannon buried in flowers," said his great admirer, Robert Schumann, of the music of Chopin.

EXPLANATION OF LISTINGS

Only currently available LP recordings are discussed in the following discographies, unless specifically noted otherwise. Recent years have seen the discontinuance of many fine discs; this is especially true of Schumann. But when a discontinued recording is of unusual musical or historical interest (Lhevinne playing Chopin; Panzéra singing Schumann), it will be mentioned. (Neither of the two widely read record catalogues is of much use in relation to cut-out records; and both of them list items that have not been available for some time. Thus they are not to be taken as infallible guides.) All records cited here are single 12-inch discs unless otherwise stated; the 10-inch classical LP has about vanished from the American record scene. The quality of recorded sound can be taken to be good unless otherwise noted. Exceptionally brilliant or exceptionally inferior examples of recorded sound will, however, be specifically mentioned.

No stereophonic recordings are discussed. Naturally all of the monophonic LP recordings discussed in the following pages can be played on a stereophonic machine. Stereophonic reproduction, in any case, is no help to a solo instrument or solo voice. It can make it larger than life, entirely unnatural; and it might be a good idea to cut out one speaker when playing the Schumann or Chopin piano music and songs. Several of the items in the following discographies already have been duplicated on stereophonic discs. A good rule to follow when considering the stereo versions is that orchestral music will be greatly helped by the second channel, solo music might actually be hurt. Considerations of interpretation, of course, remain the same for the monophonic disc and its stereophonic equivalent. In any case it is extremely difficult to tell the difference between a good monophonic orchestral record played through two speakers and a stereophonic equivalent. And a great performance remains a great performance, whether it be stereophonic, monophonic LP, or acoustic.

Piano and Orchestral Works

ANDANTE SPIANATO AND POLONAISE, FOR PIANO
AND ORCHESTRA, OP. 22
(*The Polonaise composed in 1830-31; the Andante Spianato, for solo piano, added in 1834*)

A frequent concert-hall visitor in its solo piano form, this brilliant and effective work is seldom heard in its original scoring. As Chopin composed it, the Andante Spianato (*spianato* means "smoothed-out" or "even") is a work for solo piano immediately followed by a polonaise in E-flat for piano and orchestra. The first section is a graceful piece of cantabile writing over an incessantly arpeggiated bass; the polonaise, rather long for its material, is flashy, extremely difficult technically, and has a very attractive, melancholy, middle section. Frugoni's is the only available LP version (an inept performance by Reinhardt, also on Vox, has been withdrawn). He plays nimbly enough, but not very subtly; it's all pretty much one-dimensional, with a prevailing hard tone and a lack of musical aristocracy. His disc, however, includes several rarely heard concerted pieces by Chopin, and collectors may want to investigate it. His version is uncut. Clear recorded sound, perhaps a bit too close-up. ——Orazio Frugoni; Pro Musica Orchestra, Hans Swarowsky, cond. Vox PL 9030 (with *Krako-viak; Variations on "Là ci darem la mano"; Liszt: Totentanz*)

CONCERTO FOR PIANO AND ORCHESTRA No. 1, IN E MINOR, OP. 11
(*Composed in 1830*)

Although called No. 1, the E minor Concerto was really the second in order of composition, and followed the F minor by about a year, but it was the first to be published. It is one of the composer's youthful works, and the very open-ing bears a startling relationship to the opening of Hummel's Piano Concerto in A minor. Chopin probably had the Hummel in mind. But Hummel is left far behind. The first two movements of the E minor are written by the pianist (Chopin) for the pianist (also Chopin), and it is safe to say that in 1830 he was the only man in Europe who could have played them, so new were the pian-istic concepts. In the slow movement Chopin re-veals a type of harmonic and decorative luxuri-ance that no composer in history up to then had even started to conceive. Chopin was to grow in stature and musical intensity, but the actual keyboard layout and technical invention of the

E minor Concerto was something that he never, basically, improved upon. The last movement is an example of his Polish nationalism (the two previous movements are "absolute"). As in most Chopin works for piano and orchestra, the orchestration is rather primitive: a few sticks upon which to hang the brilliant keyboard writing. But while the orchestration is tentative, it serves its purpose, and is to be preferred to the over-thick arrangements some tasteless orchestrators have lavished upon it.

Of current performances, Rubinstein remains the old master. Despite the presence, especially in the second movement, of a labored quality not normally associated with his playing, Rubinstein brings to the music more color, strength and flexibility than any of his competitors. His phrasing and his use of rubato are immensely authoritative, and there is nothing of a pink-tea quality in his virile approach. Beautiful recorded sound, though the balance between piano and orchestra leaves something to be desired; the piano is too much in the foreground.

The Uninsky performance is strong, forthright and vigorous, but without the poetry that Rubinstein brings. Uninsky, always hugely competent, sounds detached and outside the music. But even more detached is Gulda, who is so objective in his approach that he ends up being noncommittal. Horszowski is slender, tasteful, rather innocuous. He plays with more care than spontaneity, and some of the passagework gives him trouble. Fair recorded sound, too thick and muddy in the bass. Badura-Skoda's playing is also tasteful, but it is tensionless. The young Austrian carefully outlines the lyric qualities of the concerto, but he entirely misses another important aspect—its brilliance and virtuosity. Playing the notes is not enough; the concerto needs a pianist of dash and daring. Sandor's disc is impossible to recommend. He plays in a percussive, driving manner that lacks charm and flexibility. The Musulin disc has some points of interest, in that it offers both of the Chopin concertos at a low price in competent though never inspired performances. Musulin, whoever she may be (this, apparently, is her only domestic record), is not a big technician and has trouble with the nasty E major section of the first movement; but she does feel the style and she plays with honesty. She enjoys excellent recorded sound, with an especially vibrant piano tone. The François disc one can dismiss as merely eccentric. Rhythmic instabilities and technical sloppiness on this order cannot be condoned, no matter what kind of temperament the pianist may possess.

——Artur Rubinstein; Los Angeles Philharmonic, Alfred Wallenstein, cond. RCA Victor LM 1810

——Alexander Uninsky; Hague Philharmonic,

Willem van Otterloo, cond. Epic LC 3012

——Branka Musulin; Stuttgart Süddeutsche Radfunk Orchestra, Karl Mueller-Kray, cond. Period SHO 306 (with *Concerto No. 2*)   Note: Formerly Period 574.

——Paul Badura-Skoda; Orchestra of the Vienna State Opera, Artur Rodzinski, cond. West-minster XWN 18288 (with *Concerto No. 2*) or XWN 18458 (with Schumann: *Piano Concerto in A minor*) Note: Both Chopin concertos originally released on Westminster WL 5308.

——Friedrich Gulda; London Philharmonic Orchestra, Sir Adrian Boult, cond. London LL 1001

——Mieczyslaw Horszowski; Vienna State Philharmonia, Hans Swarowsky, cond. Vox PL 7870 (with *4 Impromptus*)

——Gyorgy Sandor; Philadelphia Orchestra, Eugene Ormandy, cond. Columbia ML 4651

——Samson François; Paris Conservatory Orchestra, Georges Tzipine, cond. Angel 35168 (with Liszt: *Piano Concerto No. 1*)

Concerto for Piano and Orchestra No. 2,
in F minor, Op. 21
(*Composed in 1829*)

In many respects the Second Concerto (really the first in order of composition) has many points of similarity with the E minor: the two "absolute" movements followed by a nationalistic finale; the slender orchestration; the extremely difficult and effective writing for the piano; the abundance of lyric ideas and the richness of the harmonies. It is almost impossible to resist the exuberance of the writing. But, exuberant as it is, it is extremely elegant, and no sledge-hammered virtuoso can slam his way through it. Fortunately several pianists have brought to the score the requisite combination of refinement, imagination and technical resource. The Rubinstein is a transfer of a shellac set made in 1947, and it remains a fine-sounding recording with only a slight surface to mark its source. Rubinstein's is the brightest, healthiest performance, large-scaled and full of vitality. His gorgeous tone is the perfect vehicle for the concerto. Novaes is more personal, playing with her usual poetry, freedom, and instinct for just the right degree of shading. Her recording, made in 1951, is clear but rather thin. One has the feeling that she and Klemperer do not always see eye to eye on essential details. Nevertheless, by virtue of some exquisite details, this is a performance to treasure. Ashkenazy's performance is interesting. He plays with remarkable accuracy and pliability, and with a melting tone. The only thing that mars his performance is a lack of focus: the ability to point up sharply a phrase in the authoritative manner of a Novaes or Rubinstein. That will come (the young Russian pianist was about twenty years old when he recorded the concerto in Warsaw). But so beautiful is the piano playing itself, and so sensitive the conception, that the performance, despite its occasional flabby moments, must be placed near the top of the list. The recorded sound, unfortunately, leaves much to be desired.

None of the other versions has much to offer. Malcuzynski's disc, with its mannerisms, and with an eccentric performance of the F minor Fantasy, is not recommended. Badura-Skoda lacks *élan*. Was there ever a Teutonic pianist who achieved much success with Chopin? Musulin is more convincing stylistically, and I have heard much worse Chopin playing from pianists of far greater reputation. Her resources do not match those of Rubinstein, Novaes or Ashkenazy, but if you insist on a version with both concertos on one disc, this is preferable to the Badura-Skoda, and much cheaper. Tipo's performance lacks subtlety. She piles into the F minor as though she were angry with it, playing with outsized accents and a hard tone. Her technique is clear and well regulated, but this kind of approach is anything but romantic. Pennario's superficial approach has a certain hard brilliance to recommend it, but he seldom penetrates below the surface of the music, nor is his tone capable of much nuance. The Brailowsky-Munch collaboration features routine playing, with the pianist methodically hitting the notes and the conductor hurrying along as though he were eager to get it over with. Everything is accurate enough, but the flavor of the music scarcely comes through.

——Artur Rubinstein; NBC Symphony, William Steinberg, cond. RCA Victor LM 1046

——Guiomar Novaes; Vienna Symphony Orchestra, Otto Klemperer, cond. Vox PL 7100

——Vladimir Ashkenazy; Warsaw Philharmonic Orchestra, Zdislaw Gorzynski, cond. Angel 35403 (*with Ballade No. 2 in F, Op. 38; Scherzo No. 4 in E, Op. 54; Étude No. 15 in F, Op. 25, No. 3; Mazurkas: Nos. 29 in A-flat, Op. 41, No. 4, and 21 in C-sharp minor, Op. 30, No. 4*)

——Branka Musulin; Stuttgart Süddeutsche Radfunk Orchestra, Karl Mueller-Kray, cond. Period SHO 306 (with *Concerto No. 1*)   Note: Formerly Period 574.

——Paul Badura-Skoda; Orchestra of the Vienna State Opera, Artur Rodzinski, cond. Westminster XWN 18288 (with *Concerto No. 1*)   Note: Formerly Westminster WL 5308.

——Maria Tipo; Bamberg Symphony Orchestra, Jonel Perlea, cond. Vox PL 10320 (with Schumann: *Piano Concerto in A minor*)

——Leonard Pennario; Concert Arts Orchestra, Vladimir Golschmann, cond. Capitol P 8366 (with Liszt: *Piano Concerto No. 1*)

——Alexander Brailowsky; Boston Symphony,

Charles Munch, cond. RCA VICTOR LM 1871
(with Saint-Saëns: *Piano Concerto No. 4*)

——Witold Malcuzynski; Philharmonia Orchestra, Paul Kletzki, cond. ANGEL 35030 (with *Fantasy in F minor*)

KRAKOVIAK, FOR PIANO AND ORCHESTRA, OP. 14
(*Composed in 1828*)

Some of us, early in 1950, came to admire the Vox disc of the *Krakoviak* as played by one Rosl Schmid and an orchestra conducted by Alfons Dressel. It was a cut version, however, and not very lively in sound. For some time it has been discontinued from the Vox catalogue. The present replacement, also from Vox, naturally enjoys the benefit of more up-to-date recording techniques. One wonders why this attractive score has been so neglected. In general layout and feeling it resembles the finales of the two piano concertos—objective, pianistically glittering, strongly nationalistic (a *krakoviak* is a Polish dance in duple time), immensely effective. The orchestration is no better or no worse than the orchestration in the concertos. As a purist I blush to say it, but the two cuts that were adopted in the early recording actually help the work. Schmid excised two lengthy sections of empty display passages (generally Chopin's flashy virtuoso passages in the early works can lift the listener from his seat when played well, but these

in the *Krakoviak* are among the few that are
genuinely boring). Frugoni plays the work in
its entirety. He plays competently—much better
than in the *"Là ci darem" Variations* on the same
disc—and has a strong grasp of the notes. The
performance, too, sounds better rehearsed. But
this is not my idea of idiomatic Chopin playing. Frugoni seems too intent on emphasizing the
surface glitter, and his tone does not seem capable
of much nuance. Schmid was a much more convincing exponent of the score. Nevertheless, as
indicated, the playing is competent, and those
who investigate the disc will come up with a
charming novelty that may not be encountered
in a lifetime of concert-going.

——Orazio Frugoni; Pro Musica Orchestra, Hans
Swarowsky, cond. Vox PL 9030 (with *Andante
Spianato and Polonaise; Variations on "Là ci
darem la mano"*; Liszt: *Totentanz*)

VARIATIONS ON "LÀ CI DAREM LA MANO,"
FOR PIANO AND ORCHESTRA, OP. 2
(*Composed in 1827*)

This is the work that introduced Chopin to
Robert Schumann, with the resultant famous
"Hats off, gentlemen, a genius!" It was originally
scored for piano and orchestra, though it sometimes finds its way to the concert stage as a solo
piano piece (and has been so recorded by Robert
Goldsand). Schumann saw in it "flower eyes,

basilisk eyes, peacock eyes, maidens' eyes; in many places it looked yet brighter—I thought I saw Mozart's *Là ci darem la mano* wound through a hundred chords, Leporello seemed to wink at me, and Don Juan hurried past in his white mantle. . . . Genius burns in every measure." There indeed is genius in the piece, though it has turned out to be one of the most dated works of Chopin. But what a remarkable Op. 2! Some of the keyboard writing is coruscating, and one can understand Schumann's excitement upon coming across this new language. Frugoni plays the entire set of variations, without a cut. It is not a successful attempt. His pianism has little charm or flair, while some of the variations, such as the third, are little more than a scramble. The supporting orchestra sounds thin. There is room for a version of the score in its concerted form, but this does not fill the bill.

——Orazio Frugoni; Pro Musica Orchestra, Hans Swarowsky, cond. Vox PL 9030 (with *Krakoviak; Andante Spianato and Polonaise;* Liszt: *Totentanz*)

Solo Piano Works

ALLEGRO DE CONCERT, IN A, OP. 46
(*Composed in 1840-41*)

Despite its late date of composition, the Allegro de Concert is one of the very few weak works of Chopin's maturity. He may have had Liszt in mind; a salon-like theme is used, around which all kinds of technical didos are assorted. Brilliant, but not very gratifying. Pianists have been avoiding the work through the years, and it practically never turns up in concert. Arrau's performance is mechanically expert and a little dry, though it is hard to see exactly what can be done with such an uncommunicative piece of writing.

——Claudio Arrau. ANGEL 35413 (with *Études, Op. 10*)

ANDANTE SPIANATO AND POLONAISE,
FOR SOLO PIANO, OP. 22
(*The Polonaise composed in 1830-31; the Andante Spianato added in 1834*)

See remarks above about the version of this work for piano and orchestra, as originally composed.

Most listeners will be familiar with the Andante
Spianato and Polonaise in its solo piano form.
The Andante Spianato in both versions is played
by the solo piano. It leads directly into the
Polonaise. Some pianists play a reduction of the
orchestral tutti that precedes the entrance of
the solo piano, others proceed directly to the
entrance itself. On records are two tremendous
interpretations and one transcendental one. Hofmann's is the latter. His ideas are entirely original, yet completely natural-sounding, and the
more one hears the performance, the more it
strikes fire. It is one of the greatest feats ever
captured on a piano record, and it manages to
make all other versions sound thick. In the Andante Spianato, Hofmann's tempo is considerably
faster than that of Rubinstein or Horowitz, and
the melodic line sings in an almost disembodied
manner. His treatment of the bass, too, gives a
more solid underpinning than elsewhere can be
heard, with a few deftly accented inner voices to
provide a touch of variety. His tempo in the
Polonaise, on the other hand, is slower than in
the two other versions. Hofmann takes "polonaise" literally as a dance form. Details come out
in his playing that are missing in the admirable
but more orthodox work of Horowitz and
Rubinstein (although Hofmann takes a cut, while
the other two pianists play the complete work).
Hofmann is incomparably elegant here, and

the accuracy of his fingerwork is unbelievable. The lightness and celerity of his runs, the sparkle of his arpeggio work and the dynamism of his palette are things that were unique to Hofmann. Above all was his ability to make the piano sing. Under Hofmann's fingers the piano had infinite shades of tonal nuance, like a great singer or violinist in an extended cantabile phrase. Not even the inferior quality of the recorded sound (it was made at Hofmann's golden jubilee concert, at the Metropolitan Opera on November 28, 1937) can hide the pianist's gold and silver.

Both of the Victor recordings are excellent examples of high-fidelity piano sound. Both, too, are splendid performances. Horowitz's is a little more tense, exceptionally brilliant, sharply outlined. Rubinstein's is broadly conceived, massive in conception, colorful in attack. You can't go wrong on either of these. But looming above them is the magnificence of the Hofmann.

——Josef Hofmann. COLUMBIA ML 4929 (with *"Minute" Waltz No. 6, in D-flat, Op. 64, No. 1; Ballade No. 1, in G minor, Op. 23; Berceuse, Op. 57; Nocturne No. 5, in F-sharp, Op. 15, No. 2; "Butterfly" Étude No. 21, in G-flat, Op. 25, No. 9; Nocturne No. 2, in E-flat, Op. 9, No. 2;* Rachmaninoff: *Prelude in G minor, Op. 23, No. 5;* Mendelssohn: *Spinning Song, Op. 67, No. 4;* Beethoven-Liszt: *Turkish March;* Moszkowski: *Caprice Espagnole*)

——Vladimir Horowitz. RCA Victor LM 1137 (with *Waltz No. 3, in A minor, Op. 34, No. 2; Polonaise No. 6, in A-flat, Op. 53; Mazurka No. 7, in F minor, Op. 7, No. 3; Waltz No. 7, in C-sharp minor, Op. 64, No. 2*)

——Artur Rubinstein. RCA Victor LM 2049 (with *Polonaise No. 7, in A-flat, Op. 61; Mazurkas: Nos. 22, in G-sharp minor, 23 in D, 24 in C, and 25 in B minor, Op. 33, Nos. 1-4; 26, in C-sharp minor; 27 in E minor; 28 in B, and 29 in A-flat, Op. 41, Nos. 1-4; 30 in G, and 31 in A-flat, Op. 50, Nos. 1 and 2*) NOTE: The Andante Spianato and Polonaise is also available as a filler in Rubinstein's three-disc set of the complete Mazurkas, LM 6109. It was originally recorded as 10-in. LM 152, now withdrawn.

BALLADES (4, COMPLETE)
(No. 1, in G minor, Op. 23, composed 1831-35; No. 2, in F, Op. 38, composed 1836-39; No. 3, in A-flat, Op. 47, composed 1840-41; No. 4, in F minor, Op. 52, composed in 1842)

Huneker used to divide the composer into what he called the "greater" and the "lesser" Chopin. The four Ballades are the "greater" Chopin. Did Chopin have a program in mind? He once played the F major Ballade to Schumann, who later recollected: "I remember very well that when Chopin played the Ballade here, it finished in F major; it now closes in A minor. He then said that he had been inspired by some poems of [Adam] Mickiewicz to write this Ballade." Huneker was sure that Chopin had some extra-musical associations in his head. "That Chopin had a programme, a definite programme, there can be no doubt; but he has, wise artist, left us no clue beyond Mickiewicz's, the Polish bard's Lithuanian poems." Each of the four Ballades is in six-four or six-eight time, each has a short, deliberate introduction, each is surcharged with drama, lyricism and wild outbursts. The construction in each is rather loose, but it "works." Nos. 1, 3 and 4 are extremely popular. The passionate No. 2, with its frenzied outbursts, is not played too often. One reason is its extreme difficulty. The three others are difficult enough, but No. 2 poses some phenomenal technical problems. It is one of Chopin's magnificent pieces, while No. 4 in F minor ranks with the F minor Fantasy in the opinions of many Chopinists as the greatest work he ever composed.

I am not happy with any of the current discs that offer the four Ballades in their entirety. The Casadesus version, which was released in 1950, is probably the best. But Casadesus, a superlative technician, tends to get a little away from the music, refusing to be involved too strongly. Fire and passion are missing, and not all of Casadesus' elegance can compensate. His disc has clear, rather thin recorded sound, but quite serviceable.

Cor de Groot plays steadily and methodically. Obviously he is an experienced and expert pianist. His performances have no errors of commission; but, then again, not much in the way of imagination. This is big, throbbing, pulsating music, and it simply will not offer itself to a pianist lacking in daring and wild imagination. De Groot's recording has, like many early Epics, a thudding bass.

These are the best of a none too stimulating lot. Doyen's playing is impossibly affected, a model of swooning adolescence. Arrau's performance I find excessively mannered and unnatural. He sounds calculated and his effects do not come off. He favors drawn-out ritards that start measures before Chopin indicated, he constantly changes the metrical pulse, and his rubato creaks. Technique he has. The recorded sound is full, clear, and a little hard. Frugoni rattles through the music with the impersonality of an auditor checking a balance sheet, and Jambor has trouble playing some of the notes. In the coda to the F minor Ballade she about halves the tempo, and even then she does not come through unscathed. Technical considerations aside, her view of the Ballades leaves much to be desired.

——Robert Casadesus. Columbia ML 4798 (with *Sonata No. 2, in B-flat minor, Op. 35*)

——Cor de Groot. Epic LC 3037 (with *Berceuse, Op. 57; Nocturne No. 5, in F-sharp, Op. 15, No.*

2; *"Minute" Waltz No. 6, in D-flat, Op. 64, No. 1; Waltz No. 7, in C-sharp minor, Op. 64, No. 2*)

——Ginette Doyen. WESTMINSTER XWN 18037 NOTE: Originally released as WL 5169.

——Claudio Arrau. In DECCA DXB 130, 2 discs (with *4 Impromptus; 4 Scherzos; Barcarolle*)

——Agi Jambor. CAPITOL P 8403 (with *4 Impromptus*)

——Orazio Frugoni. Vox PL 10490 (with *4 Impromptus*)

BALLADES (INDIVIDUAL)

No. 1, in G minor, Op. 23. Probably the most-played of the four Ballades, the G minor is a combination of lyricism and power that represents Chopin at his best. Hofmann's recording is the one that best catches the lyricism and power. Again the recorded sound is inferior, but who cares? Hofmann is heroic and delicate in turn, with more color and authority than anybody who has attempted the work on discs. One hears a degree of imagination that vanished when Hofmann died. In the Barere disc, the piano tone is not bad, but the recording is low-level and has prominent surfaces. Barere brings a mannered quality to his reading. He tinkers around with the opening phrases, altering the note values and in general has some arbitrary notions that do not always come off. Yet there is never any doubt that an extraordinary pianist (as contrasted to musician) is at work, and there are some ravishing details. Barere had amazing pianistic fluency. He was one of the supreme technicians of this or any other age, and in addition he could employ a very warm and subtly colored tone. Intellectually, however, his playing is apt to be on the surface. The Horowitz disc is a transfer to LP of shellac 78-rpm discs made in 1948: dated sound, boomy bass. His performance has excitement, but it is also finicky, extremely tight and sometimes actually disconnected. One extremely effective, and even tremendous moment: the crash in the bass in the measure preceding the beginning of the coda.

Throughout his career, Backhaus has been interested in Chopin (his early recording of both books of études, about 1927, was a landmark in its day) and he obviously has a great admiration for the Polish composer. And yet his Chopin playing has never been convincing. This performance of the G minor Ballade is typical. It is well planned, and Backhaus' wonderful fingers clarify all of the notes, but the elements of rapture, of improvisation and color, are missing. The playing is too inflexible. Janis, the young American pianist, also suffers from too sober an approach. He is an intelligent artist, and his clear playing is always in the best of taste. Missing is personality. A pianist even younger than Janis, the Frenchman Philippe Entremont, does supply that quality of personality. Entremont is extremely talented. In addition to being a finished keyboard workman, he has an instinctive feeling for romantic music, and his disc of the Ballade is a fine contribution to the Chopin discography. The recorded sound, however, is tinny and leaves much to be desired. In Anda's disc, the G minor Ballade fills out the last side of the Chopin Études (Op. 10). He plays in a languishing, sentimental manner. This is the kind of Chopin interpretation that gives the composer a bad name.

——Josef Hofmann. COLUMBIA ML 4929 (with *"Minute" Waltz No. 6, in D-flat, Op. 64, No. 1; Berceuse, Op. 57; Nocturne No. 5, in F-sharp, Op. 15, No. 2; "Butterfly" Étude No. 21, in G-flat, Op. 25, No. 9; Nocturne No. 2, in E-flat Op. 9, No. 2; Andante Spianato and Polonaise, for solo piano, Op. 22;* Rachmaninoff: *Prelude in G minor, Op. 23, No. 5;* Mendelssohn; *Spinning Song, Op. 67, No. 4;* Beethoven-Liszt: *Turkish March;* Moszkowski: *Caprice Espagnole*)

——Simon Barere. REMINGTON R 17 (with *Scherzo No. 3, in C-sharp minor, Op. 39;* Liszt: *Liebestraum; Gnomenreigen;* Gounod-Liszt: *Faust Waltz*)

——Vladimir Horowitz. RCA VICTOR LM 1235 (with *Sonata No. 2, in B-flat minor, Op. 35; Nocturne No. 5, in F-sharp, Op. 15, No. 2;* Liszt:

Au bord d'une source; Hungarian Rhapsody No. 6)

——Philippe Entremont. CONCERT HALL CHS 1502 (with *Polonaise No. 6, in A-flat, Op. 53; Nocturne No. 4, in F, Op. 15, No. 1; Waltzes: Nos. 6, in D-flat, and 7, in C-sharp minor, Op. 64, Nos. 1 and 2; 13, in D-flat, Op. 70, No. 3; 9, in A-flat, Op. 69, No. 1; 3, in A minor, Op. 34, No. 2; and 5, in A-flat, Op. 42; Mazurka No. 32, in C-sharp minor, Op. 50, No. 3; Scherzo No. 3, in C-sharp minor, Op. 39*)

——Wilhelm Backhaus. LONDON LL 1556 (with *Mazurkas: Nos. 24, in C, Op. 33, No. 3; 20, in D, Op. 30, No. 3; and 17, in B-flat minor, Op. 24, No. 4; Waltz No. 2, in A-flat, Op. 34, No. 1; Études: Nos. 2, in A minor; 3, in E; 5, in G-flat; 8, in F; 10, in A-flat, Op. 10, Nos. 2, 3, 5, 8, and 10; 13, in A-flat; 14, in F minor; 15, in F; 18, in G-sharp minor; 19, in C-sharp minor; 20, in D-flat; 21, in G-flat; and 23, in A minor, Op. 25, Nos. 1, 2, 3, 6, 7, 8, 9, and 11*) NOTE: The G minor Ballade was originally issued on 10-in. LPS 317, now withdrawn.

——Byron Janis. RCA VICTOR LM 2098 (with *Waltzes: Nos. 3, in A minor, Op. 34, No. 2; and 14, in E minor, posth.; Étude No. 8, in F, Op. 10, No. 8;* Liszt: *Liebestraum, Hungarian Rhapsody No. 6;* Brahms: *4 Waltzes, Nos. 15, 1, 2, and 6;* Strauss-Schulz-Evler: *On the Beautiful Blue Danube*)

——Geza Anda. ANGEL 35420 (with *12 Études, Op. 10*)

No. 2, in F, Op. 38. The fiery F major Ballade (which, incidentally, ends in the unrelated key of A minor) is one of the great explosions in the Chopin literature. It is true that the piece starts quietly enough, and it ends with a plaintive sigh, but in between come the *Presto con fuoco* sections in which the piano positively erupts. Here a pianist needs wrists of steel and fingers with a built-in telescope at each tip. Of the two recorded versions, that of Ashkenazy is far more convincing. He may lack some of the tigerish strength that the Ballade needs, but he does have style, a knowledge of the idiom and a fantastic ability to get over the keys. This boy should develop into a great pianist. Malcuzynski is nowhere near the technician that Ashkenazy is, nor does he have the quality of melting tone that his younger colleague possesses. In addition, Malcuzynski has some curious ideas, with strange holds in the *Presto con fuoco,* a lack of basic rhythmic pulse and no particular elegance to the phrasing. His is a better-sounding recording, with clear piano reproduction, but Ashkenazy's disc is serviceable despite its lack of bell-like clarity.

——Vladimir Ashkenazy. ANGEL 35403 (with *Piano Concerto No. 2, in F minor, Op. 21;*

*Scherzo No. 4, in E, Op. 54; Études: Nos. 1, in C,
Op. 10, No. 1; and 15 in F, Op. 25, No. 3;
Mazurkas: Nos. 21, in C-sharp minor, Op. 30, No.
4; and 29, in A-flat, Op. 41, No. 4)*

——Witold Malcuzynski. ANGEL 35171 (with
*Nocturnes: Nos. 7, in C-sharp minor, Op. 27, No.
1; and 15, in F minor, Op. 55, No. 1; Waltzes:
"Minute," No. 6, in D-flat, Op. 64, No. 1; and
11, in G-flat, Op. 70, No. 1; Mazurkas: Nos. 21,
in C-sharp minor, Op. 30, No. 4; 45, in A minor,
Op. 67, No. 4; and 25, in B minor, Op. 33, No.
4; Impromptu No. 1, in A-flat, Op. 29; Scherzo
No. 2, in B-flat minor, Op. 31)*

No. 3, in A-flat, Op. 47. The lightest, prettiest,
most graceful of the four Ballades. None of the
current LP versions is entirely satisfactory.
Katchen is brash, immature, and all on the surface. He is in many respects an amazing virtuoso,
but it all sounds misplaced here. The Horowitz
pressings I played had a prominent scratch
throughout. Otherwise the recorded sound is
exceptionally clear. This is a big performance,
with plenty of art and artifice, but it does not
sound natural. Horowitz misses the grace and
elegance of the music, and there are some odd
sections involving detached finger weights.
Nearly everything sounds too *big*. Of course the
pianistics proper are beyond reproach. Entremont disappoints. His playing is not as relaxed

as it is on his Concert Hall disc; he is slow, careful and occasionally drips sentiment. At least the Demus version is tasteful, well-planned and accurately delivered. It does not offer much of an emotional experience, but it probably is the performance closest to Chopin's intentions.

——Joerg Demus. WESTMINSTER XWN 18723 (with *Nocturnes: Nos. 5, in F-sharp, Op. 15, No. 2; and 18, in E, Op. 62, No. 2; Prelude, in C-sharp minor, Op. 45; Nouvelle Étude No. 3, in D-flat; Impromptu No. 3, in G-flat, Op. 51;* and pieces by Schumann, Brahms, Debussy and Demus)

——Vladimir Horowitz. RCA VICTOR LM 1707 (with *Ballade No. 4, in F minor, Op. 52; Nocturnes: Nos. 19, in E minor, Op. 72, No. 1; and 15, in F minor, Op. 55, No. 1; Scherzo No. 1, in B minor, Op. 20; Impromptu No. 1, in A-flat, Op. 29; Études: Nos. 3, in E; and 4, in C-sharp minor, Op. 10, Nos. 3 and 4*)

——Julius Katchen. LONDON LL 1325 (with *Scherzo No. 3, in C-sharp minor, Op. 39; Fantasy, in F minor, Op. 49;* Brahms: *Variations and Fugue on a Theme by Handel*) NOTE: The Chopin works on this disc were originally issued on 10-in. LS 554, now discontinued.

——Philippe Entremont. EPIC LC 3316 (with *Nocturne No. 8, in D-flat, Op. 27, No. 2; Impromptu No. 1, in A-flat, Op. 29; Tarantelle, Op. 43; Scherzo No. 1, in B minor, Op. 20; Polonaises: Nos. 5, in F-sharp minor, Op. 44; and 3, in A, Op. 40, No. 1*)

No. 4, in F minor, Op. 52. The F minor Ballade
is Chopin at his very peak. It is packed full of
drama and unforgettable melodic ideas. Certainly
the opening theme following the short introduction is one of the supreme lyric inventions of the
romantic movement. Horowitz starts his performance beautifully, with a singing line and a
firmly shaped contour. Then he becomes capricious: he adds little crescendi and diminuendi
that testify to his pianistic control and his interest in pianistic effects rather than his interest in
the broad sweep of the music itself. Withal, some
thrilling playing, including a triumphal negotia-
tion of the coda (one of the most difficult in the
repertory). Superb recorded sound.

——Vladimir Horowitz. RCA Victor LM 1707
(with *Ballade No. 3, in A-flat, Op. 47; Nocturnes:
Nos. 19, in E minor, Op. 72, No. 1; and 15, in F
minor, Op. 55, No. 1; Scherzo No. 1, in B minor,
Op. 20; Impromptu No. 1, in A-flat, Op. 29;
Études: Nos. 3, in E; and 4, in C-sharp minor,
Op. 10, Nos. 3 and 4*)

BARCAROLLE, IN F-SHARP, OP. 60
(Composed in 1845-46)

Some very great pianists have recorded the
Barcarolle, one of the lushest, most richly har-
monized and melodious of Chopin's works. It
is a fairly long, and extremely difficult, work
with an incessantly rocking bass that is intended,
undoubtedly, to represent the rocking of the

waters in a Venetian canal. But there is nothing really Italianiate about the Barcarolle, which is a prime example of Chopin's sophisticated cosmopolitanism. Some fine recordings are available. Lipatti takes the phrases between his hands and carefully shapes them. A masterful performance, one with nobility, passion and tremendous control. The 1948-ish recording has a thick sound. Try the 78-rpm equalization with reduced bass. Horowitz, in his performance, is massive, exciting, and nervous-sounding. It is thrilling to hear this kind of pianistic finesse, but there is something too agitated, too lacking in emotional repose, in the playing. Uninsky and Firkusny play clearly, without frills. Both offer sensible, sensitive, expert performances. Balogh is delicate and small-scaled. It is impossible to recommend the Pennario or Arrau discs. Pennario has power but he sounds crude, and the beauty in the music seems to mean little to him; while Arrau is so mannered that he ends up sounding eccentric. Gieseking always loved the Barcarolle (he had made a prior recording, in the 1930's), and never achieved too much success with it. Despite his subtlety of tone and ability to color a phrase, his approach is too cut-and-dried. The Banhalmi disc is competent—and lacking in personality. Banhalmi, however, offers quite a few almost unknown Chopin pieces, in their only LP recordings, and thus his disc is valuable.

——Dinu Lipatti. Columbia ML 4721 (with *Sonata No. 3, in B minor, Op. 58; Nocturne No. 8, in D-flat, Op. 27, No. 2; Mazurka No. 32, in C-sharp minor, Op. 50, No. 3*)

——Vladimir Horowitz. RCA Victor LM 2137 (with *Scherzos: Nos. 2, in B-flat minor, Op. 31; and 3, in C-sharp minor, Op. 39; Nocturnes: Nos. 3, in B, Op. 9, No. 3; 4, in F, Op. 15, No. 1; 7, in C-sharp minor, Op. 27, No. 1; and 2, in E-flat, Op. 9, No. 2*)

——Rudolf Firkusny. Capitol PAO 8428 (with *Scherzo No. 2, in B-flat minor, Op. 31; Nocturnes: Nos. 2, in E-flat, Op. 9, No. 2; and 8, in D-flat, Op. 27, No. 2; Waltzes: Nos. 1, in E-flat, Op. 18; and 7, in C-sharp minor, Op. 64, No. 2; Polonaise No. 4, in C minor, Op. 40, No. 2*)

——Alexander Uninsky. Epic LC 3122 (with *Fantasy, in F minor, Op. 49; Mazurkas: Nos. 17, in B-flat minor, Op. 24, No. 4; 40, in F minor, Op. 63, No. 2; 23, in D, Op. 33, No. 2; 13, in A minor, Op. 17, No. 4; 27, in E minor, Op. 41, No. 2; and 48, in C-sharp minor, Op. 68, No. 3; Nocturnes: Nos. 1, in B-flat minor, Op. 9, No. 1; and 8, in D-flat, Op. 27, No. 2*)

——Erno Balogh. Lyrichord LL 20 (with *4 Impromptus; Bolero, Op. 19; Berceuse, Op. 57; Tarantelle, Op. 43*)

——Walter Gieseking. Angel 35501 (with Mozart: *Piano Concerto No. 24, in C minor, K. 491*)

——George Banhalmi. Vox PL 10370 (with *Variations on a German Air; Tarantelle, Op. 43; Nocturne in C-sharp minor, posth.; Rondo in E-flat, Op. 16; Prelude in A-flat, posth.; Prelude in C-sharp minor, Op. 45; Variations Brillantes, Op. 12; Bolero, Op. 19*)

——Leonard Pennario. CAPITOL L 8246. 10-in. (with Liszt: *Mephisto Waltz*)

——Claudio Arrau. DECCA DXB 130, 2 discs (with *4 Ballades; 4 Impromptus; 4 Scherzos*)

BERCEUSE, IN D-FLAT, OP. 57
(*Composed in 1843*)

A berceuse is a cradle song. As Chopin has written it, the piece is a *tour de force*. The left hand maintains virtually the same bass figuration (including, often, the same harmonies) throughout the entire work, while the right hand is given opportunities for extravagant decoration. There is something almost Italianate about the writing, and Chopin probably had the vocal lines of his adored Bellini in mind. This *Berceuse* is a slight, elegant and almost hypnotic work, and it demands a pianist with extraordinary suppleness. Those rippling scale passages and elaborate ornamentations are far from easy. To Novaes go the honors for a shimmering, poetic reading. Her technique is a little rougher than one normally hears from her, but the quality of interpretation is lovely. Hofmann's ideas are strange, and this is the one piece on his disc that fails to convince. The tempo is fast, he does not seem particularly interested in the music (bored?), and the accented A-flats toward the end sound arbitrary. De Groot is, as always, dependable, sensible and not very imaginative. Balogh's performance neither adds much to the music nor takes anything away. One could do much worse. Nadas, for example, is thick and heavy, and his slow tempo makes the work disintegrate. Frugoni is loud and insensitive, and he makes this delicate *Berceuse* sound like an étude.

——Guiomar Novaes. Vox PL 7810 (with *Scherzo No. 3, in C-sharp minor, Op. 39; "Minute" Waltz No. 6, in D-flat, Op. 64, No. 1; Impromptu No. 2, in F-sharp, Op. 36; Nocturne No. 5, in F-sharp, Op. 15, No. 2; Fantasy, in F minor, Op. 49; Étude No. 3, in E, Op. 10, No. 3*)

——Josef Hofmann. Columbia ML 4929 (with *"Minute" Waltz No. 6, in D-flat, Op. 64, No. 1; Ballade No. 1, in G minor, Op. 23; Nocturnes: Nos. 5, in F-sharp, Op. 15, No. 2; and 2, in E-flat, Op. 9, No. 2; "Butterfly" Étude No. 21, in G-flat, Op. 25, No. 9; Andante Spianato and Polonaise, Op. 22;* Rachmaninoff: *Prelude in G minor, Op. 23, No. 5;* Mendelssohn: *Spinning Song, Op. 67, No. 4;* Beethoven-Liszt: *Turkish March;* Moszkowski: *Caprice Espagnole*)

——Cor de Groot. Epic LC 3037 (with *4 Ballades; Waltzes: "Minute," No. 6, in D-flat; and*

7, *in C-sharp minor, Op. 64, Nos. 1 and 2*)

——Erno Balogh. LYRICHORD LL 20 (with *4 Impromptus; Bolero, Op. 19; Barcarolle, Op. 60; Tarantelle, Op. 43*)

——Istvan Nadas. PERIOD 722 (with *Preludes: "Raindrop," No. 15, in D-flat; and 24, in D minor, Op. 28, Nos. 15 and 24; Polonaise No. 6, in A-flat, Op. 53; Scherzo No. 2, in B-flat minor, Op. 31; Nocturne No. 5, in F-sharp, Op. 15, No. 2; Études: No. 3, in E; "Black Key," No. 5, in G-flat; "Revolutionary," No. 12, in C minor, Op. 10, Nos. 3, 5, and 12; and "Butterfly," No. 21, in G-flat, Op. 25, No. 9; "Military" Polonaise No. 3, in A, Op. 40, No. 1; Fantasy-Impromptu, in C-sharp minor, Op. 66; Mazurkas: Nos. 13, in A minor, Op. 17, No. 4; and 14, in G minor, Op. 24, No. 1; "Minute" Waltz No. 6, in D-flat, Op. 64, No. 1*)

——Orazio Frugoni. Vox PL 10510 (with *4 Scherzos; 3 Ecossaises*)

BOLERO, IN C, OP. 19
(*Composed in 1833*)

A fluffy, pianistic and not too interesting trifle that seldom turns up in concert. Minor Chopin, energetically played by Balogh and Banhalmi. The latter has better quality of recorded sound, and the contents of his disc contain the only LP recordings of several works.

——George Banhalmi. Vox PL 10370 (with

Variations on a German Air; Tarantelle, Op. 43; Nocturne in C-sharp minor, posth.; Prelude in A-flat, posth.; Prelude in A-flat, Op. 45; Rondo in E-flat, Op. 16; Variations Brillantes, Op. 12; Barcarolle, Op. 60; Berceuse, Op. 57)

——Erno Balogh. LYRICHORD LL 20 (with *4 Impromptus; Berceuse, Op. 57; Tarantelle, Op. 43*)

ECOSSAISES (3), OP. 72
(*Composed in 1826*)

Lightweight music, a product of Chopin's youth (he was sixteen). The writing is immature, the content shallow. But at that, the *Ecossaises*, or "Scotch Dances," are as good examples of salon music as anybody was writing at the time. Mauro-Cottone presents the best of the two available versions (an older one by Dorfmann has been withdrawn by Victor). She is clear, accurate and tasteful, and she does not try to make too much out of the music. Frugoni is nimble-fingered but lacks Mauro-Cottone's grace.

——Aurora Mauro-Cottone. KAPP 9012 (with encore pieces)

——Orazio Frugoni. Vox PL 10510 (with *4 Scherzos; Berceuse*)

ÉTUDES (24, COMPLETE)
(*The first book of Études, Op. 10, Nos. 1-12, was composed between 1829-32; the second book, Op. 25, Nos. 1-12, between 1832-36.*)

If Bach's *Well-Tempered Clavier* is the pianist's Bible, the two books of Chopin études are his New Testament. The études explore every aspect of piano technique as it was known at that time (and precious little has been added since the publication of Op. 25). Each étude poses a specific technical problem ("étude" means "study"). No. 1 is devoted to right-hand arpeggios; No. 2 to the last three fingers of the right hand; No. 3 to legato phrasing; and so on. There are studies devoted to thirds, sixths, and double notes in general; to broken chords; to staccato; to cross-rhythms; to arpeggiated chords, and other devices. But never is there a lapse in inspiration. As in the *Preludes*, each of these little sketches is a musical world in itself, cunning in its workmanship, wonderfully tooled, imaginative in conception. Chopin dedicated the set to Liszt, probably the only pianist in Europe, aside from the composer himself, who could have played them correctly at the time.

It takes a Protean pianist to tackle the Chopin études, with their diversity of mood and variety of technical problems. Unfortunately, no such artist has attempted the task. Two pianists—Uninsky and Brailowsky—have recorded both books as a unit. Uninsky takes one disc for the two books. Brailowsky, on two discs, also plays Schumann's *Études symphoniques* and Chopin's *Trois nouvelles études*. Uninsky's is the preferable version, though he leaves much to be desired. There is something essentially earthbound in his approach, and while he has a competent grasp of the notes, he does little to vitalize them. And in some cases his ideas are highly debatable, to say the least, especially the affectations he brings to the more lyric of the études. Brailowsky goes through the music with a percussive attack, a finger equipment not up to all of the demands imposed by the music, and a lack of variety in dynamics. Generally his playing is too loud; and once he arrives at a specific dynamic level, it takes little short of an earthquake to get him out.

——Alexander Uninsky. Epic LC 3065

——Alexander Brailowsky. RCA Victor LM 6000, 2 discs (with *Trois nouvelles études;* Schumann: *Études symphoniques*)

ÉTUDES, OP. 10 (12, COMPLETE)
(*Composed between 1829-32*)

Here, and in Op. 25, Novaes is responsible for some of her strangest playing on LP. My guess is that she had not looked at some of these études for many years before whipping them into shape for the recording session. In any case her work is erratic and often not up to par technically. I prefer Goldsand, who does not rise to Novaes' great moments but is steadier all-around. His tempos, a trifle deliberate, suggest that he approached the music with the determination not to take any chances. As a result, we get disciplined readings that never let themselves go. Excitement is lacking; but better this than anarchy. Excellent recorded sound. Arrau, a wonderful technician, gives what amounts to a blueprint—clear and exact (as is the recorded sound on his disc), yet somehow uninteresting, without the flair, color and flexibility (not to mention the poetry) that the great Chopinists have brought to the music. Compare his picky, awkward-sounding version of the arpeggiated E-flat Étude with Lhevinne's performance on CAMDEN CAL 265 (now, alas, withdrawn). Lhevinne is all grace, suppleness, color, subtlety; while Arrau's rubato sounds like a hiccup. Nor can the Slenczynska disc be recommended. She turns in some vigorous playing, but hers is an immature style, and she does some things that are incomprehensible. It is a pity that Victor has never transferred to microgroove the only great performance of Op. 10 ever released in America, the Cortot version of 1938.

——Robert Goldsand. CONCERT HALL H 1632 (with *Trois nouvelles études*)   NOTE: This disc was originally released as CHS 1132.

——Guiomar Novaes. Vox PL 9070 (with Chopin: *Scherzo No. 1, in B minor, Op. 20*)

——Claudio Arrau. ANGEL 35413 (with *Allegro de Concert, Op. 46*)

——Ruth Slenczynska. DECCA DL 9890 (with

Impromptu No. 1, in A, Op. 29; Impromptu No. 2, in F-sharp, Op. 36)

ÉTUDES, OP. 25 (12, COMPLETE)
(*Composed between 1832-1836*)

See remarks above. Novaes is below her usual form, and the steadier Goldsand is preferred. Neither Arrau nor Slenczynska improve upon their performances in the Op. 10 set. The new entrant is Anda, who in this recording of Op. 25 attains a respectable level. In music as coruscating as this, however, something more than a respectable level is needed, and Anda does not supply it. He takes a sensible view toward the music, has a good technique, and he even supplies a welcome bit of color at times—but never does he make a memorable experience of any of the études.

——Robert Goldsand. CONCERT HALL H 1633 (with *Trois nouvelles études*) NOTE: This disc was originally released as CHS 1133.

——Guiomar Novaes. Vox PL 7560 (with *Trois nouvelles études*)

——Geza Anda. ANGEL 35420 (with *Ballade No. 1, in G minor, Op. 23*)

——Claudio Arrau. ANGEL 35414 (with *Trois nouvelles études*)

——Ruth Slenczynska. DECCA DL 9891 (with *Impromptu No. 3, in G-flat, Op. 51; Fantasy-Impromptu, in C-sharp minor, Op. 66*)

ÉTUDES, COMPOSED AFTER THE METHOD
OF FÉTIS (TROIS NOUVELLES ÉTUDES)
(*Composed in 1839*)

These three short, agreeable and salon-like pieces
were written at the invitation of Ignaz Moscheles
(an important pianist-composer of the day) and
included in a publication by Moscheles and
François Joseph Fétis (music theorist and his-
torian) named *Méthode des méthodes*. Four
pianists have recorded them as fillers in their
discs of études. Novaes and Goldsand rate
highest. The keys of the three études are F
minor, A-flat and D-flat. Demus has recorded
the D-flat alone, and quite nicely on WESTMIN-
STER XWN 18273. See entry under Ballade No. 3
for complete contents of the Demus disc.

——Robert Goldsand. CONCERT HALL H 1632
(with *Études, Op. 25*)

——Guiomar Novaes. VOX PL 7560 (with
Études, Op. 25)

——Claudio Arrau. ANGEL 35414 (with *Études,
Op. 25*)

——Alexander Brailowsky. RCA VICTOR LM
6000, 2 discs (with *Études, Op. 10 and 25;* Schumann: *Études symphoniques*)

ÉTUDES (COLLECTIONS AND MISCELLANEOUS)

All styles of Chopin playing are represented by
the pianists discussed alphabetically below. There

is the Slavic way of playing Chopin—with much rubato, a juicy tone, considerable rhythmic (and, sometimes, even textual) freedom, and all kinds of color devices. There is the French way— tonally brilliant, elegant, metrically quite regular, shallow in tone, coloristically restricted. There is the German way—square, methodical, as rhythmically regular as the French but considerably heavier. The Germans play Chopin with the air of a bishop at a junior prom, determined to be a good sport about it all.

Ashkenazy represents the Slavic way. On ANGEL 35403 (with *F minor Concerto and solo miscellany*) he plays the C major (Op. 10, No. 1) and F major (Op. 25, No. 3) Études. These are remarkable. Only a handful of living pianists could match the degree of precise articulation he achieves; and yet this is not a stunt, for the playing has elegance and refinement. Backhaus, on LONDON LL 1556, can be heard in thirteen études (along with the G minor Ballade and other Chopin pieces). He has selected from Op. 10 the following: Nos. 2, 3, 5, 8 and 10; and from Op. 25, Nos. 1-3, 6-9 and 11. As an executant he is still one of the most formidable mechanisms before the public. Yet his magnificent fingerwork sounds square. Even when he toys with the meter he manages to sound square. If you want a dignified, clear, unhurried and unperfumed Chopin, Backhaus is your man. But the Slavic way will remain the choice of most aficionados. Badura-Skoda, on WESTMINSTER XWN 18281 (a disc devoted to piano encores), plays the popular E major (Op. 10, No. 3) and C-sharp minor (Op. 25, No. 7) Études in a rather limp and unexhilarating manner. Gorodnitzki, in the *Butterfly* Étude (Op. 25, No. 9), on CAPITOL P 8374 (a disc of encores) is routine. An amazing *Butterfly* is offered by Hofmann on COLUMBIA ML 4929 (Andante Spianato and Polonaise, etc.). Listen to the lightness and crispness of the attack, and the startling decrescendo in the middle section, not to mention the incisive accentuations. On VICTOR LM 1707 (F minor Ballade, etc.), Horowitz plays the E major (Op. 10, No. 3) in a rather mannered fashion and then whizzes through the following C-sharp minor Étude (Op. 10, No. 4) with grand virtuosity. Janis is one of several who plays the *Black Key* Étude (Op. 10, No. 5); he can be heard in a deft performance on VICTOR LM 2091 (Sonata in B-flat minor, etc.). A discontinued disc, CAMDEN 265, contains Josef Lhevinne's great performances of the *Winter Wind* Étude (Op. 25, No. 11), the E-flat (Op. 10, No. 11), the *Étude in Thirds* (Op. 25, No. 6) and the octave Étude in B minor (Op. 25, No. 22). If you ever run across this disc, grab it. Contained in its grooves is some of the most stylish Chopin playing ever recorded. Istvan Nadas, on PERIOD 722, plays the E major, *Black*

Key, *Revolutionary* (Op. 10, No. 12) and *Butterfly* Études, and these are among the best performances on an otherwise puzzling record. Nadas obviously is a good technician, but he seems so determined to avoid virtuoso glitter that his playing ends up stodgy. In these études, however, he is under firm technical and rhythmic control. See listing under Scherzo No. 2 for the full contents of the Nadas disc. Novaes, in her disc of Chopin pieces (Vox PL 7810), has a rather routine performance of the E major (see listing under Scherzo No. 3 for full contents of the Novaes disc). A Paderewski reissue, CAMDEN 310, contains several études—the *Revolutionary*, *Black Key* and C-sharp Minor (Op. 25, No. 7), played in a grand style that the acoustic recorded sound cannot hide. A pair of discs of short encores presents Pennario in hard-driven performances of the *Black Key* (CAPITOL P 8338) and E major (CAPITOL P 8391) Études.

Altogether a novelty, not the Chopin études but allied to them, are the Godowsky paraphrases that David Saperton plays on KAPP KCL 9013. Godowsky took many of the Chopin études and combined them. He juggled together the *Black Key* and *Butterfly*, for example—both études are in the key of G-flat—and named the result *Badinage*. These paraphrases are ingenious, near-impossible to play because of their extreme difficulty and contrapuntal complexity, and are virtually out of fashion today. Saperton, Godowsky's son-in-law, makes a brave attempt, and the very fact that he gets through without a breakdown is cause enough for congratulations.

FANTASY, IN F MINOR, OP. 49
(*Composed 1840-41*)

Many specialists call the F minor Fantasy Chopin's greatest work. It has everything—a spacious design, amazingly rich harmonies, melodic content of a varied nature, unity in variety. A slow chorale section bisects the work; it is reminiscent somewhat of the quasi-*religioso* sections of some of Liszt's piano music. The F minor Fantasy gives the lie to Field's statement that Chopin's was "a sickroom talent." It is virile and passionate music, from the mysterious introduction to the striding march just before the coda. But Chopin is not only at his strongest here. He also is at his most lyrical, and one of his supreme inspirations is the long-phrased theme in thirds and sixths that occurs three times.

Heading the top of the LP list is Novaes. Despite a few awkward moments, she brings to the music a typical combination of personality, color and poetry. She never lags, and neither does she strain to attain heroic flights. She presents the music within a modest framework, but within that framework she is all nuance. The recorded sound is faithful enough to convey the subtlety of her tone. Uninsky is more direct than Novaes. He plays with fine musicianship and admirable technical control, although he just misses a full realization of the poetic content (especially in the ravishing A-flat section). Strong and assured playing nevertheless. Not much can be said of the other versions. Katchen's performance is a glib collection of pianistic effects rather than a unified conception. Malcuzynski's ideas I find merely eccentric. Right at the opening he goes his own way, ignoring Chopin's indications; and his rubato is of a type that (as they say in the used car ads) must be heard to be appreciated.

——Guiomar Novaes. Vox PL 7810 (with *Scherzo No. 3, in C-sharp minor, Op. 39; "Min-ute" Waltz No. 6, in D-flat, Op. 64, No. 1; Impromptu No. 2, in F-sharp, Op. 36; Nocturne No. 5, in F-sharp, Op. 15, No. 2; Étude No. 3, in E, Op. 10, No. 3; Berceuse, Op. 57*)

——Alexander Uninsky. Epic LC 3122 (with *Mazurkas: Nos. 17, in B-flat minor, Op. 24, No. 4; 40, in F minor, Op. 63, No. 2; 23, in D, Op. 33, No. 2; 13, in A minor, Op. 17, No. 4; 27, in E minor, Op. 41, No. 2; and 48, in C-sharp minor, Op. 68, No. 3; Barcarolle, Op. 60; Nocturnes: Nos. 1, in B-flat minor, Op. 9, No. 1; and 8, in D-flat, Op. 27, No. 2*)

——Julius Katchen. London LL 1325 (with *Scherzo No. 3, in C-sharp minor, Op. 39; Ballade No. 3, in A-flat, Op. 47; Brahms: Variations and Fugue on a Theme by Handel*) NOTE: The Chopin items on this disc were originally released as 10-in. LPS 554.

——Witold Malcuzynski. ANGEL 35030 (with *Concerto No. 2, in F minor, Op. 21*)

FANTASY-IMPROMPTU, IN C-SHARP MINOR, OP. 66. *See* Impromptus
IMPROMPTUS (3); FANTASY-IMPROMPTU

(*No. 1, in A-flat, Op. 29, composed in 1837; No. 2, in F-sharp, Op. 36, composed in 1839; No. 3, in G-flat, Op. 51, composed in 1842. The Fantasy-Impromptu, in C-sharp minor, Op. 66, was composed in 1834 but published posthumously.*)

Chopin composed four impromptus. The fourth, and most popular—indeed, one of Chopin's all-time favorites, along with the Waltz in C-sharp minor and the *Funeral March*—is the so-called Fantasy-Impromptu. Chopin called it an impromptu; the "fantasy" part was tacked on by a publisher. It is the weakest of the four, with a simpering middle section that goes on and on and on. Schumann admired the A-flat Impromptu no end, and was a little puzzled by it. The composition, he thought, "so little resembles anything in the whole circle of his works that I can scarcely compare it with any other Chopin composition; it is so refined in form, its cantilena from beginning to end so enclosed in charming figuration." No. 2, in F-sharp, has even more elaborate figuration. The concluding section, indeed, is a tropical growth of exquisite running passages. But never display passages; the filigree here is an essential part of the melodic line. No. 3, in G-flat, is seldom played. One wonders why. It is the most introspective of the four, exceedingly graceful, and by far the richest harmonically.

No really satisfactory version of the complete set exists, although some splendid versions of individual impromptus are available (see following entry). Balogh's is the best. His playing is neat, accurate and tasteful. What it lacks is a degree of musical personality. Yet surely it is preferable to Arrau's sighings and intellectualized emotionalism. Arrau simply pulls the F-sharp Impromptu to pieces. His recording is clear but a little glassy. Balogh's, though thin, is satisfactory. In his recording, Horszowski is conscientious, but that is not enough. These pieces are above all improvisatory. Horszowski's sober process of presenting the notes without commenting on them leaves an important element out. His recording has a fine sound in the treble, a soggy thump in the bass. Frugoni rattles through the music, quite missing its lyricism and elegance, while Jambor is deficient in style.

——Erno Balogh. LYRICHORD LL 20 (with *Bolero, Op. 19; Berceuse, Op. 57; Tarantelle, Op. 43; Barcarolle, Op. 60*)

——Mieczyslaw Horszowski. Vox PL 7870 (with *Concerto No. 1, in E minor, Op. 11*)

——Claudio Arrau. DECCA DXB 130, 2 discs (with *4 Scherzos; 4 Ballades; Barcarolle, Op. 60*)

——Orazio Frugoni. Vox PL 10490 (with *4 Ballades*)

——Agi Jambor. CAPITOL P 8403 (with *4 Ballades*)

IMPROMPTUS (INDIVIDUAL)

No. 1, in A-flat, Op. 29. The most impressive performance on LP comes from Horowitz, on RCA VICTOR LM 1707 (Chopin recital): a carefully shaped interpretation, articulated with all of Horowitz' infernal wizardy. The evenness of his passage work is frightening. Janis, on another VICTOR disc (LM 2091, with other Chopin pieces), plays dependably and with a streak of poetry. Kentner's disc, CAPITOL P 8400 (Chopin and Liszt), reveals the work of an experienced pianist. Some of his ideas are debatable, but they nevertheless have authority. Entremont, on EPIC LC 3316 (Chopin recital), is talented but not as convincing as he can be. Slenczynska (DECCA 9890: Chopin recital) and Malcuzynski (ANGEL 35171: Chopin recital) are not convincing at all.

No. 2, in F-sharp, Op. 36. Surprisingly enough, only two recordings. Novaes, in Vox PL 7810 (Chopin recital) has it all over Slenczynska, in

DECCA 9890 (Chopin recital). The great lady is in superb form here, singing out the opening melody; and the subsequent fioritura is just made for her fingers. Alongside this kind of cultivated art of glints and shadings, Slenczynska sounds stiff.

No. 3, in G-flat, Op. 51. Entremont is best here. His version, in CONCERT HALL CHS 1502 (Chopin recital), is a shade fast but elegant and flexible. Demus, in WESTMINSTER XWN 18723 (recital), supplies a good, steady performance. Slenczynska (DECCA 9891) imposes some arbitrary notions on the music.

No. 4, in C-sharp minor, Op. 66 (Fantasy-Impromptu). Two fine performances of this work are available. One is played by Rubinstein on RCA VICTOR LM 1153 (recital), who turns in the kind of singing, masculine, athletic (in the best sense of the word) interpretation that is expected of him. The other is contained in a recently discontinued disc, CAMDEN 348 (recital), played by Harold Bauer. Bauer made regrettably few recordings, and this disc helps tell why his cultured art was held in such respect. Kentner, in CAPITOL P 8400 (Chopin and Liszt) is steady and reliable. Pennario (CAPITOL P 8391: recital) is brilliant but tonally hard to the point of percussiveness. So is Lewenthal in WEST-

MINSTER XWN 18403 (recital). Slenczynska (DECCA 9891: Chopin recital) and Nadas (PERIOD 722: Chopin recital) bring up the rear.

MAZURKAS (COMPLETE)

(Most editions contain 51 mazurkas. The order of opus numbers and dates of composition are as follows: Op. 6, Nos. 1-4, composed in 1830-31; Op. 7, Nos. 1-5, 1830-31; Op. 17 Nos. 1-4, 1832-33; Op. 24, Nos. 1-4, 1834-35; Op. 30, Nos. 1-4, 1836-37; Op. 33, Nos. 1-4, 1837-38; Op. 41, Nos. 1-4, 1838-39; Op. 50, Nos. 1-3, 1841; Op. 56, Nos. 1-3, 1843; Op. 59, Nos. 1-3, 1845; Op. 63, Nos. 1-3, 1846; Op. 67, Nos. 1-4, 1835 for Nos. 1 and 3, 1846 for No. 4 and 1849 for No. 2; Op. 68, Nos. 1-4, 1829 for Nos. 1 and 3; 1827 for No. 2 and 1849 for No. 4. In addition there is an A minor Mazurka, identified as "dedicated to Émile Gaillard, 1841; and another A minor Mazurka, named "Notre temps," composed in 1840.)

The mazurka is a Polish dance in three-four rhythm, and it represents Chopin's most extended flight into nationalism. He composed over fifty of these little dances (little in size; some of them are epic in emotional scope), from the time he was a student in Warsaw until the end of his life. "Chopin," wrote Schumann, "has elevated the mazurka to a small art form. He has written many, yet few among them resemble each other. Almost every one contains some poetic trait, something new in form and expression." Schumann singled out the Mazurka No. 20, in D-flat, Op. 30, No. 3, as an example of writing "which will make German cantors throw up horrified hands above scandalized heads." The mazurka ends in parallel fifths, which, as Schumann points out, "the great theorists forbade under pain of death." He wisely, and farsightedly (for his day), adds that parallel fifths should be judged in context with the composition.

In pre-war days, only one pianist was brave enough—and, from Victor's standpoint, popular enough—to take on the entire series. That was Artur Rubinstein, and his original recording, issued around 1940 in three albums, was one of the glories of the pre-war repertoire. His current three-disc LP set is not a transfer but a new recording. It is difficult to think of a living pianist to whom the mazurkas could be more safely entrusted. As Rubinstein plays the music, it emerges with all its nostalgia and exoticism, all its emotional health and bounding rhythm. No affectations are present, no gilding the lily, none of the calculated superimpositions that mar the work of so many of his colleagues. More than any pianist alive, Rubinstein expresses a *joie de vivre* in his playing. Here it is, captured for posterity. The Victor engineers were most cooperative in this release, giving Rubinstein clear, undistorted recorded sound. What results is a basic

item for any collection of Chopin, and also one
of the all-time great piano recordings. Magaloff
is unfortunate in finding himself up against this
album. His three-disc set is competently played,
but it lacks the character of Rubinstein's, and the
interpretations sound tame, lacking in tension and
tonal resource.

——Artur Rubinstein. RCA Victor LM 6109, 3
discs (with *Andante Spianato and Polonaise, Op.
22; Polonaise-Fantasy, Op. 61*)

——Nikita Magaloff. London A 4329, 3 discs

MAZURKAS (COLLECTIONS)

Several pianists have contributed discs devoted
entirely or in large part to Chopin mazurkas.
Here is a breakdown. Horowitz plays seven:
Nos. 20, 21, 26, 32, 38, 40 and 41. Kapell, on
Victor LM 1715, plays nine: Nos. 9, 14, 24, 25,
35, 44, 45, 48 and 49; and on LM 1865, he plays
seventeen: Nos. 2, 6, 11, 12, 20, 22, 26, 27, 31,
32, 36, 37, 40, 41, 43, 47 and 50. Novaes is heard
in twelve: Nos. 13, 15, 17, 23-26, 34, 36, 37, 39
and 51. Malcuzynski plays eight: Nos. 7, 15, 17,
20, 27, 32, 41 and 47. Uninsky plays six: Nos. 13,
17, 23, 27, 40 and 41. The Horowitz disc is very
interesting. He plays with a carefully turned line,
with simplicity, sensitivity and his usual remarkable control. He is heard to excellent advantage
here, and the delicacy of his work, plus a thorough identification with the style, makes this

disc one of his great ones (the Schumann *Kinderscenen* on the reverse is also beautifully delivered). Novaes is more personal, more fragrant and scented. Many listeners do not like this disc, and it has been described as wayward. All I can say is that I continue to listen to it with delight. Kapell, in his two discs, is a little tight, but he plays with taste and understanding, and with remarkable finger control. His second disc, LM 1865, is better than its predecessor, with a singing line and considerable musical flow. One slight defect: in the A-flat Mazurka, Op. 17, No. 3, there is a faulty tape snip. Uninsky plays with clarity, and just a shade of dryness. But his able presentation and thorough musicianship make his disc a recommended one. Malcuzynski goes about it with a hard tone and a stop-and-start rubato that is too exaggerated for comfort.

The Rubinstein disc is one of the three in his complete recording. It has been separately issued because it contains the two polonaises on the reverse. Naturally it is very much worth owning, and those who do not wish to invest in the three-disc set could very well start with it as a sampler.

——Vladimir Horowitz. Seven Mazurkas. RCA VICTOR LVT 1032 (with Schumann: *Kinderscenen*) NOTE: This disc was originally released as LM 1109

——Artur Rubinstein. Nine Mazurkas. RCA VICTOR LM 2049 (with *Andante Spianato and*

Polonaise, Op. 22; Polonaise-Fantasy, Op. 61)

——William Kapell. Nine Mazurkas. RCA VICTOR LM 1715 (with *Sonata No. 3, in B minor, Op. 58)*

——William Kapell. Seventeen Mazurkas. RCA VICTOR LM 1865

——Guiomar Novaes. Twelve Mazurkas. Vox PL 7920

——Alexander Uninsky. Six Mazurkas. EPIC LC 3122 (with *Fantasy, in F minor, Op. 49; Barcarolle, Op. 60; Nocturnes: Nos. 1, in B-flat minor, Op. 9, No. 1; and 8, in D flat, Op. 27, No. 2)*

——Witold Malcuzynski. Eight Mazurkas. ANGEL 35284 (with *Polonaises: Nos. 4, in C minor, Op. 40, No. 2; 5, in F-sharp minor, Op. 44; and 6, in A-flat, Op. 53)*

MAZURKAS (INDIVIDUAL)

Many pianists have recorded individual mazurkas on discs devoted to a miscellany of music. Let's take them alphabetically. Ashkenazy plays two on his Chopin disc (ANGEL 35403)—Nos. 21, in C-sharp minor, Op. 30, No. 4; and No. 29, in A-flat, Op. 41, No. 4. These are delicate, sensitive performances, very much in the Polish idiom. Backhaus plays three (17, in B-flat minor, Op. 24, No. 4; 20, in D-flat, Op. 30, No. 3, and 24, in C, Op. 33, No. 3) in an unyielding, Germanic manner on LONDON LL 1556 (Chopin recital). A clear and elegant performance of No. 32, in C-sharp minor, Op. 50, No. 3, is supplied by Entremont on CONCERT HALL CHS 1502 (Chopin recital). Horowitz, on RCA VICTOR LM 1137 (Chopin recital) plays No. 7, in F minor, Op. 7, No. 3; and on VICTOR LM 1957 (recital) can be heard in No. 17, in B-flat minor, Op. 24, No. 4. Both performances are pianistically impeccable and stylistically convincing. Horowitz' pupil, Janis, plays No. 45, in A minor, Op. 67, No. 4, with direct simplicity on RCA VICTOR LM 2091 (Chopin recital). The great Mazurka No. 32, in C-sharp minor, Op. 50, No. 3, is magnificently played by Lipatti on COLUMBIA ML 4721. Malcuzynski, on ANGEL 35171 (Chopin recital), plays three—Nos. 21, in C-sharp minor, Op. 30, No. 4; 25, in B minor, Op. 33, No. 4; and 45, in A minor, Op. 67, No. 4; and on ANGEL 35348 (recital) he can be heard in No. 47, in A minor, Op. 68, No. 2. These are heavily accented performances that try to stress the dance elements. Nadas, on PERIOD 722 (Chopin recital) is tasteful and unhurried in Nos. 13, in A minor, Op. 17, No. 4, and 14, in G minor, Op. 24, No. 1. In the same A minor that Nadas plays, and also in No. 25 in B minor, Op. 33, No. 4, Zecchi is extremely sentimental and affected (WESTMINSTER XWN 18139: recital).

NOCTURNES (COMPLETE)
(Most editions contain nineteen nocturnes. The order of opus numbers and dates of composition are as follows: Op. 9, Nos. 1-3, 1830-31; Op. 15, Nos. 1-3, 1830 for Nos. 1 and 3, 1833 for No. 3; Op. 27, Nos. 1-2, 1834-35; Op. 32, Nos. 1-2, 1836-37; Op. 37, Nos. 1-2, 1838-39; Op. 48, Nos. 1-2, 1841; Op. 55, Nos. 1-2, 1843; Op. 62, Nos. 1-2, 1846; Op. 72, No. 1, 1827.)

Several of the nocturnes—the E-flat of Op. 9, the F-sharp and the D-flat—number among Chopin's most popular works. They were recorded ad infinitum in acoustic days and still have a large representation on LP discs. The nocturnes, like the waltzes, represent the salon side of Chopin, and most of them are dainty, dreamlike and superficial. At least two, however—the C minor and C-sharp minor—are compositions on the grand scale; and the subtle E major Nocturne is a pastel with wonderful spots of color.

Rubinstein's performance holds its eminence. Not much can be said here that wasn't said in reference to Rubinstein's performance of the mazurkas (see above). In these nocturnes he brings an equivalent degree of strength, poetry and technical finesse. He achieves the sentiment of the music without ever becoming sentimental, and the way he sings out the melodic content is an object lesson for all pianists. Rubinstein remains the romantic *par excellence*. He has been given superb recorded sound. The Novaes performance is quite lovely. She does not have Rubinstein's control and unfaltering rhythm—not in this set, at any rate—but hers is imaginative and altogether lovely playing, with that liquid quality of tone and phrase so typical of the pianist. Where Novaes is delicate and rhythmically flexible, Reisenberg is inclined to be metronomic and objective: a noonday sun against a moonlit night. Reisenberg's accurate playing is something to admire. She is a fine musician and an extraordinarily finished pianist. But her very accuracy and insistence on rhythmic regularity make her interpretations sound just a shade pedantic and overworked. Katin too is a fine musician who ends up, in these nocturnes, lacking in spontaneity. There is more color to the music than he brings out. Smeterlin gives us a perfumed, sentimental Chopin; and Smeterlin, in addition, is not the complete master of the notes. Brailowsky is dry, and Istomin stomps through the music without much feeling for niceties of style.

——Artur Rubinstein. RCA Victor LM 6005, 2 discs. Also available separately on LM 2175 (Vol. I) and LM 2176 (Vol. II).

——Guiomar Novaes. Vox PL 9632, 2 discs. Also available separately on PL 9632/1 (Vol. I) and 9632/2 (Vol. II).

——Nadia Reisenberg. WESTMINSTER XWN 18256/18257

——Peter Katin. LONDON LL 1281 (Vol. I) and LL 1499 (Vol. II)

——Alexander Brailowsky. RCA VICTOR LM 2160 (Vol. I) and LM 2161 (Vol. II)

——Eugene Istomin. COLUMBIA SL 226, 2 discs. Also available separately on ML 5054 (Vol. I) and ML 5055 (Vol. II).

——Jan Smeterlin. EPIC 3151 (Vol. I) and 3152 (Vol. II)

NOCTURNES (INDIVIDUAL)

Again let's take an alphabetical look at some of the pianists who have recorded individual nocturnes. Banhalmi, on Vox PL 10370 (Chopin recital), gives the only LP performance of the early Nocturne in C-sharp minor, which Chopin named *Lento con gran' espressione*. It was composed in 1830 and uses a few themes from the F minor Piano Concerto. Banhalmi plays expertly. Cor de Groot has recorded the popular F-sharp Nocturne (Op. 15, No. 2) on EPIC LC 3037 (Chopin recital), playing carefully and steadily. Demus, on WESTMINSTER XWN 18273 (recital), also plays the F-sharp, as well as the lovely E major, Op. 62, No. 2, and he handles his assignment with skill. Entremont, on CONCERT HALL CHS 1502 (Chopin recital), is simple and tasteful in the F major, Op. 15, No. 1; but in the

D-flat Nocturne, on Epic LC 3316 (Chopin recital), he sounds much too heavy. Firkusny, in his Chopin recital on Capitol PAO 8428, is heard in cultured performances of the E-flat Nocturne, Op. 9, No. 2, and D-flat, Op. 27, No. 2, Josef Hofmann's incomparable performances of the E-flat and F-sharp can be heard on Columbia ML 4929 (recital). Horowitz has scattered nocturnes through several of his discs. On RCA Victor LM 1235 (Chopin and Liszt) he offers a handsome performance of the F-sharp; on LM 1707 (Chopin recital) he is at his worst in the F minor, Op. 55, No. 2, and E minor, Op. 72, No. 1. The F minor is impossibly mannered. A better version of the E minor is contained in Horowitz' twenty-fifth anniversary album, RCA Victor LM 6014, two discs. Still another Horowitz disc, LM 2137 (Chopin recital), contains the Nocturnes in B, Op. 9, No. 3; F, Op. 15, No. 1; C-sharp minor, Op. 27, No. 1, and E-flat; Op. 9, No. 2. Immensely powerful, but too taut, playing. Janis plays the D-flat quite nicely on RCA Victor LM 2091 (Chopin recital). Kentner also turns in a fine D-flat on Capitol P 8400 (Chopin and Liszt). Lewenthal's performances of the E-flat and F-sharp, on Westminster XWN 18403 (recital) are routine. A beautifully spun-out D-flat is contributed by Lipatti on Columbia ML 4721 (Chopin recital), whereas Malinin in his D-flat, on Angel 35396 (Rachmaninoff) is orthodox and not very individual. Malcuzynski, in the C-sharp minor and F minor Nocturnes (ANGEL 35171: Chopin recital), displays competence rather than imagination. The F-sharp that Nadas plays is very over-deliberate (PERIOD 722: Chopin recital) and quite the opposite Pole from Novaes' poised interpretation on Vox PL 7810 (Chopin recital). Pennario's hard approach to the E-flat Nocturne is anything but ingratiating (CAPITOL P 8338: recital). Rubinstein, in an encore disc (RCA VICTOR LM 1153), gracefully captures the essence of the E-flat Nocturne. And Uninsky's well-regulated pianism is heard to good advantage on EPIC LC 3122 (Chopin recital), where he plays the Nocturnes in B-flat Minor, Op. 9, No. 1, D-flat and the C minor, Op. 48, No. 1.

POLONAISES
(Standard editions contain the following ten polonaises: Op. 26, No. 1, in C-sharp minor, and No. 2, in E-flat minor, composed in 1834-35; Op. 40, No. 1, in A major—the "Military" Polonaise —and No. 2, in C minor, 1838-39; Op. 44, in F-sharp minor, 1840-41; Op. 53, in A-flat, 1843; Op. 61, in A-flat—the "Polonaise-Fantasy"— 1845-46; and Op. 71, No. 1, in D minor, No. 2, in B-flat, and No. 3, in F minor, composed in 1827, 1828 and 1829, respectively.)

With the mazurkas, the polonaises are Chopin's

most important excursions into nationalism. Of
the ten, the Op. 72 set, dating from Chopin's
youth, are almost never heard in concert. Nor do
the first two turn up much. The "Military" Polonaise, too, has almost dropped from the repertoire. Indeed, the A-flat Polonaise is the only
one around which pianists flock, though in recent
years the Polonaise-Fantasy, a late and rather
problematical work, has been achieving popularity. Both the A-flat and the Polonaise-Fantasy are
great works. So is the F-sharp minor, and its
relative neglect is hard to fathom. Its bravura
octave passages should, one might think, make it
a paradise for virtuoso pianists. But somehow it
has never achieved a secure place.

Ever since the Johannesen version was dropped
from the Vox catalogue, several years ago, there
has been no complete set of the polonaises.
Rubinstein's "complete" version is *not* complete.
He plays the first six and the Polonaise-Fantasy,
and also includes the Andante Spianato and Polonaise (originally composed as a work for piano
and orchestra, though generally played in a version for solo piano). The deleted Vox set (PL
6840) is worth making an attempt to locate.
Johannesen is a very able pianist, and his set not
only contains the ten polonaises but throws in
two more that were posthumously published.

Rubinstein's performances of the first seven
polonaises is exemplary. He can easily encompass

the heroic thunderings of the A-flat Polonaise as well as the gentle lyricism of the C-sharp minor. His playing has breadth and fire, unlimited virtuosity and tone color. Above all, his playing is never neurotic, and its grand line never becomes tight. In a Rubinstein performance everything sounds natural, and so it is in the polonaises.

——Artur Rubinstein. RCA Victor LM 1206 (*Polonaises 1-6*) and LM 2049 (*Polonaise-Fantasy; Andante Spianato and Polonaise; Mazurkas: Nos. 22-31*) Note: The Polonaise-Fantasy and Andante Spianato and Polonaise also are recorded as the last side of Rubinstein's 3-disc set of mazurkas, LM 6109. Both works were originally released on 10-inch LM 152.

Polonaises (individual)

No. 3, in A, Op. 40, No. 1. The so-called "Military" Polonaise, or *Polonaise Militaire.* Nadas is extremely unconventional in his recording (Period 722: Chopin recital). He wants a march-like atmosphere, and his tempo is extremely deliberate. He manages to carry it off, but one is left with the feeling that there is something unnatural about the piece as it sounds under Nadas' fingers. A more orthodox performance is contributed by Gorodnitzki on Capitol P 8374 (recital). Entremont's performance, however, on Epic LC 3316 (Chopin recital) is the most satisfactory of the single versions. He maintains a nice forward movement, and he holds his youthful strength and exuberance well under control. Inferior recorded sound, though.

No. 4, in C minor, Op. 40, No. 2. Firkusny's Chopin recital on Capitol PAO 8428 contains an intelligent performance of the C minor Polonaise. Firkusny typifies the younger generation of Chopin pianists at its best. He scrupulously observes the notes, accents and dynamic indications (unlike many of the old-timers, who took all kinds of liberties). He is an excellent technician and commands a singing tone. At the present time he is still a little too objective in his interpretations. Musical and sensitive as they are, a sense of really strong personal involvement is missing. But such poised and secure playing should evoke nothing but admiration. Malcuzynski, on Angel 35284 (Chopin recital), plays in an angular manner with hard tonal characteristics. He does have a certain feeling for the style, but his playing is singularly devoid of color.

No. 5, in F-sharp minor, Op. 44. Rubinstein, in his complete version, leaves the field far behind. Of the others, there are Entremont (Epic LC 3316: Chopin recital) and Malcuzynski (Angel 35284: Chopin recital) to consider. The Entremont version is lyric and well planned, though without the epic sweep it should have. Malcuzynski is less interesting.

No. 6, in A-flat, Op. 53. The three important
versions of this most popular of the Chopin polonaises come from Rubinstein (discussed above,
in RCA VICTOR LM 1205), Horowitz (RCA
VICTOR LM 1137: Chopin recital) and Lhevinne
(CAMDEN 265, now discontinued). Rubinstein is
exciting, beautifully organized and heroic in its
sweep. Horowitz is on a comparable level, with
mighty hammer strokes, unlimited virtuosity and
a breathless build-up. The Lhevinne is something
that should not be missed, and this Camden disc
is one of the really unfortunate deletions of the
LP era. If you ever come across it, don't hesitate;
buy! The A-flat Polonaise was one of Lhevinne's
specialties. He made this recording in 1936, and
it illustrates his combination of strength and
delicacy. It also shows off the technical equipment of one of the grandest of virtuosos (one
whose octaves, especially, were unmatched).

Of the other available versions, the best is contributed by Entremont on CONCERT HALL CHS
1502: Chopin recital), though the inferior quality of the recorded sound is a decided liability.
Pennario's impetuous performance (CAPITOL L
8156: Chopin recital) has little to recommend it,
nor is Malcuzynski (ANGEL 35284: Chopin recital) a satisfactory solution. The Nadas performance (PERIOD 722: Chopin recital) is eccentric, and it is hard to understand what he is getting at. He plays the opening at such a slow

tempo that all vitality is lost, and his rhythmic pulse varies sometimes even within the phrase.

No. 7, in A-flat, Op. 61 (Polonaise-Fantasy). To Rubinstein's brilliant version can be added that of Horowitz (RCA VICTOR LM 1957: recital). Rubinstein plays in a big, unaffected manner. Horowitz is perhaps more brilliant, but he also is tighter and more tense. A beautiful performance nevertheless, and a magnificent solution of the technical problems. The Polonaise-Fantasy is one of Chopin's late works, and it is a rather problematic one that never has achieved much popularity. Yet it is a masterpiece, and a subtle one. It has none of the directness of the previous polonaises. Rather it is almost a questioning work, full of contrast and delicacy (though it does build up to a thundering conclusion). It has been called "pathological" by some critics. Even Liszt, so sympathetic to Chopin's music, found it "feverish . . . approaching madness." The Polonaise-Fantasy is not a work that quickly unlocks its secrets, but repeated hearings should demonstrate that it is unique; and what Liszt mistook for madness is really intensity, though of a low-keyed kind.

PRELUDES, OP. 28 (COMPLETE)
(Composed 1836-39; many of them probably composed previously)

For almost all composers until Chopin, a prelude
was a short instrumental piece intended to be
played before a longer allied work (Bach's forty-
eight preludes and fugues that make up the *Well-
Tempered Clavier* are a case in point). Chopin's
Op. 28 consists of twenty-four preludes. As in
the *Well-Tempered Clavier*, there is a composition in each of the major and minor keys. But
there the relationship ends (unless Chopin intended to write fugues for his preludes: and the
idea is not as ridiculously far-fetched as it might
sound). Most of the preludes are short and improvisatory in character. A work like the C-sharp
minor Prelude, which takes only a few seconds
to play, glints briefly and vanishes. Outside of the
key relationships (Chopin followed the circle of
fifths: C major, A minor, G major, E minor, D
major, B minor, etc.), the preludes have no uni-
fying thread. Some are lyric, some heroic, some
sound fully planned, some sound like sketches.
The only thing in common is the imagination of
the respective pieces. Schumann found them
"most remarkable. I will confess that I expected
something quite different, carried out in the
grand style, like his études. It is almost the contrary here; these are sketches, the beginnings of
studies, or, if you will, ruins. . . . But in every
piece we find, in his own refined hand, written
in pearls, 'This is by Frédéric Chopin.' . . . He
is the boldest, proudest, poet-soul of today. To

be sure, the book also contains some morbid, feverish, repellant traits; but let every one look in it for something that will enchant him." One of the preludes that must have bothered Schumann no end is the strange and morbid No. 2 in A minor, as dissonant a piece as Chopin ever wrote, and as enigmatic.

No outstanding versions of the preludes has been recorded on LP. Although the Novaes dates from 1949 the sound is quite tolerable if the bass is drastically reduced. To my taste this is the best modern interpretation. Examined pedantically, some of Novaes' playing might not stand up too well, but despite some negative moments there shine through the performances her flexibility, her instinct for a telling phrase and, above all, a feeling of spontaneity that is exactly in line with the nature of the music. Rubinstein is not in the best of form on his disc. It is one of his few examples of unconvincing Chopin playing, and one hesitates to recommend a disc that has so many capricious moments. Of course, the pianist being Artur Rubinstein, there also are moments of magnificence. Cor de Groot is steady, as always, playing with a maximum of musicianship and a minimum of poetry. Gulda's disc is a fine effort. Everything is laid out in a logical manner, the fingerwork is impeccable and the musical ideas sound. But Gulda does lack color, and he is a long way from the freedom and inspiration of

Novaes. Both Arrau and Brailowsky bring a methodical approach and a lack of emotional warmth. Of the two, Arrau is the superior technician. Neither, however, even begins to suggest the romanticism of the music.

——Guiomar Novaes. Vox PL 6170
——Artur Rubinstein. RCA Victor LM 1163
——Friedrich Gulda. London LL 755
——Cor de Groot. Epic LC 3017
——Alexander Brailowsky. RCA Victor LM 1150
——Claudio Arrau. Columbia ML 4420

PRELUDE, IN C-SHARP MINOR, OP. 45
(*Composed in 1841*)

In addition to the twenty-four preludes of Op. 28, there is the C-sharp minor Prelude that was published separately in 1841. It is one of the longer preludes, and its chief interest is harmonic. The work passes from key to key in a subdued manner, and its total impression is rather negative. Despair and resignation predominate. Both recordings are eminently satisfactory. Demus and Banhalmi play with taste and with clear-cut fingerwork. The Banhalmi disc, however, is recommended, for its contains the only LP recordings of several Chopin works, while most of the Demus items on his encore disc can be duplicated elsewhere.

——George Banhalmi. Vox PL 10370 (with

Variations on a German Air; Tarantelle, Op. 43;
Nocturne in C-sharp minor, posth.; Rondo in
E-flat, Op. 16; Prelude in A-flat, posth.; Varia-
tions Brillantes, Op. 12; Bolero, Op. 19; Bar-
carolle, Op. 60)

——Joerg Demus. WESTMINSTER XWN 18273
(with *Nocturnes: Nos. 5, in F-sharp, Op. 15, No.*
2; and 18, in E, Op. 62, No. 2; Nouvelle Étude
No. 3, in D-flat; Impromptu No. 3, in G-flat, Op.
51; pieces by Schumann, Brahms, Debussy and
Demus)

PRELUDES (INDIVIDUAL)

Very few pianists have turned their attention to
single preludes. On Vox PL 10370 (Chopin recital), Banhalmi offers the only LP recording of
the posthumous A-flat Prelude, a short and
graceful work of no particular importance that
was not published until 1918. Lhevinne's discontinued CAMDEN 310 contains brilliant performances of the Preludes Nos. 17 in A-flat and 16
in B-flat minor. The latter is, with the exception
of the D minor, the most fiery of the preludes.
It was one of Lhevinne's specialties. On PERIOD
722 (Chopin recital), Nadas quietly plays Nos.
15 in D-flat and No. 4 in E minor. No. 15 is the
so-called *Raindrop* Prelude.

RONDO, IN E-FLAT, OP. 16
(*Composed in 1832*)

One of Chopin's weaker works, thematically un-distinguished, though elaborate in its layout and pianistic figurations. Banhalmi plays quite accurately and the recorded sound is excellent.

——George Banhalmi. Vox PL 10370 (with *Variations on a German Air; Tarantelle, Op. 43; Nocturne in C-sharp minor, posth.; Preludes in A-flat, posth., and C-sharp minor, Op. 45; Barcarolle, Op. 60; Variations Brillantes, Op. 12; Bolero, Op. 19*)

RONDO, IN C, FOR TWO PIANOS
(*Composed in 1828*)

An early work, effectively written for the two pianos. The theme itself is of a salon nature, but the writing is very sophisticated, and a section in the minor key more than hints at the great Chopin to come. Considering the date of composition—1828—the work is a marvel. Vronsky and Babin present a glittering performance, with all the necessary virtuosity and sparkling fingerwork.

——Vitya Vronsky and Victor Babin. DECCA DL 9790 (with Schubert: *Fantasy in F minor;* Liszt: *Concerto Pathétique;* Milhaud: *Scaramouche*)

SCHERZOS (4, COMPLETE)
(*No. 1, in B minor, Op. 20, composed in 1831-32; No. 2, in B-flat minor, Op. 31, 1837; No. 3, in*

C-sharp minor, Op. 39, 1838-39; No. 4, in E, Op. 54, 1842)

With the ballades, the scherzos are Chopin's most-played larger compositions. The first two are turbulent and heroic, and of this pair, No. 2 in B-flat minor is a stupendous outburst. A generation or so ago it was hard to attend a piano recital and not find it on the program. It remains one of Chopin's most-played works. No. 3 in C-sharp minor is almost as popular. Its dashing opening octaves create an air of excitement, and the remarkable chorale sections, in which solemn chords are decorated by sunbursts of single-note figurations, are among the most imaginative Chopin ever composed. Least-played of all is No. 4 in E, the lightest of the four. It abounds in running scale passages and is divided in half by a lovely, plaintive section in C-sharp minor. Saint-Saëns had the opening of the scherzo in mind when he came to compose the second movement of his G minor Piano Concerto.

Of the available complete versions, only one need concern us. Rubinstein, whose pre-war set of the scherzos remained unique in the catalogues, has re-recorded them with just as much style, insight and technical *expertise*. For large-scale, yet well-proportioned Chopin, he leaves all competition far behind. Next to this kind of playing, Bolet is ineffectual. An extraordinary technician, Bolet is fine when his agile fingers are in motion. When he has to pause for reflection, he obviously is not too certain what to do. Then come the hesitancies and a break-up of the line. Arrau too is a masterly technician, but he is excessively mannered. Take the B minor Scherzo, where he lets the middle section die on the vine while he strings out an interminable ritard. This kind of thing occurs too often. Uninsky is dependable but uninspired. Not much poetry comes through, and even less personality. There is an inhibited quality to the playing that is unfortunate in view of Uninsky's potentialities. Frugoni goes about his work in a dashing manner, with plenty of keyboard control. But after a while his hectic, relentless pushing-on begins to pall. There is not enough relief, not enough variety, not enough variation in dynamics. Everything sounds too loud. The Slenczynska recording is impossible to recommend. Her tempos are impossibly slow and the affectations of her phrasing become neither her nor Chopin.

——Artur Rubinstein. RCA Victor LM 1132.

——Alexander Uninsky. Epic LC 3430.

——Jorge Bolet. Remington R 161.

——Orazio Frugoni. Vox PL 10510 (with *Berceuse, Op. 57; Three Ecossaises*)

——Claudio Arrau. Decca DXB 130, 2 discs (with *4 Ballades; 4 Impromptus; Barcarolle, Op. 60*)

——Ruth Slenczynska. Decca DL 9961.

SCHERZOS (INDIVIDUAL)

No. 1, in B minor, Op. 20. Rubinstein's performance on VICTOR LM 1132 (see above) remains my first choice. Horowitz has made two recordings, one on VICTOR LM 6014 (an item in the two-disc Twenty-fifth Anniversary Album) and one on LM 1707 (Chopin recital). I prefer the former, which is somewhat slower than its companion but which is more carefully shaped and more natural-sounding. Novaes has a quite different approach on Vox PL 9070. She is, as always, the deftest of pianists; her performance is light and sure-fingered, with the lyricism of the work uppermost in mind. Unfortunately it is on a disc containing an indifferent performance of the Op. 10 Études. In his Chopin recital (EPIC LC 3316), Entremont plays the B minor Scherzo in a manner much too like a finger exercise. There is some brilliant detail, but the young French pianist here suggests that the work is still beyond him.

No. 2, in B-flat minor, Op. 31. The Horowitz performance on RCA VICTOR LM 2137 (Chopin recital) is interesting and, at the same time, unsettling. The outstanding quality of the interpretation is its sense of power: a massive, smooth-rolling pianistic mechanism almost frightening in its relentless sweep through the music. Yet with all its power and clarity, it seems denuded of color, substituting instead a tense, febrile quality. Although Horowitz follows the notes closely, even taking the *sempre con fuoco* in tempo (*everybody* broadens the tempo here), the results sound unnatural. Perhaps his insistence on making every note "sound" contributes to the unusual effect, for the usual approach is to pedal the bass line. Horowitz uses scarcely any pedal, letting his fingers do the work. For the first time everything is clearly heard; but I, for one, am not sure that this was what Chopin intended. Firkusny, in CAPITOL PAO 8248 (Chopin recital), follows the lead of Horowitz in using very little pedal and letting the fingers do the work. His is a very sound and sensitive performance that could stand a bit more temperament. Malcuzynski, in ANGEL 35171 (Chopin recital) goes in for some heavy woodchopping, and Nadas in PERIOD 722 (Chopin recital) is much too affected. Rubinstein's version in the complete set is the most satisfactory (VICTOR LM 1132).

No. 3, in C-sharp minor, Op. 39. Several excellent versions are available, including, of course, Rubinstein's, which is discussed above. Barere's fleet-fingered performance on REMINGTON R 17 (Chopin and Liszt) is extremely effective. He could be very elegant when he wanted to. Here the notes deliciously roll off his fingers, and in the coda he is sensational. Low-level recording, prominent surfaces. Novaes, on Vox PL 7810 (Chopin recital), plays with her expected imagination and flair, and with the utmost beauty of tone: a simple, exquisite, beautifully tooled performance. Horowitz strives for a linear quality, and he achieves it in a breath-taking manner on RCA VICTOR LM 2137 (Chopin recital). For sheer brilliance this is in a class by itself, though the Rubinstein (RCA VICTOR LM 1132) version is more musical. Katchen, on LONDON LL 1325, and Karl Ulrich Schnabel, on URANIA 8001, do not belong in this company of giants. Janis presents a clear, beautifully organized performance in RCA VICTOR LM 2091 (Chopin recital), and Entremont shows real flair for the music in CONCERT HALL CHS 1502 (Chopin recital), though the buyer must expect inferior recorded sound in the Concert Hall disc.

No. 4, in E, Op. 54. Aside from Rubinstein, in his complete version on RCA VICTOR LM 1132, the only interesting performance of the Fourth Scherzo comes from Ashkenazy (ANGEL 35403: Chopin recital). Beauty of tone and clarity of fingerwork mark the playing of the young Polish pianist. Ashkenazy appears, on the basis of this record, to be a pianist in the Pachmann tradition, though with a million times more musicianship and rhythmic control. This is a very impressive example of playing, all the more in that Ashkenazy was nineteen years old when he made this recording.

SONATA FOR PIANO No. 1, IN C MINOR, OP. 4
(*Composed in 1827*)

Chopin's teacher, the good Joseph Xavier Elsner, was an academician. Thus he was anxious that his gifted pupil compose academic works, such as sonatas and fugues. (Chopin did write a full-length fugue for piano; it has never been recorded.) The C minor Sonata is a product of Chopin's apprenticeship, and was undoubtedly written under Elsner's supervision. It is not a very distinguished work, though nowhere near as bad as some authorities think. The third movement, in five-four time, is sufficiently unusual; and some of the piano writing prefigures the great innovator. So far as I know, Goldsand is the only pianist since the invention of the phonograph to have recorded the C minor Sonata. His performance is faithful, accurate and uncut. Excellent recorded sound.

——Robert Goldsand. CONCERT HALL H 1650 (with *Variations on "Là ci darem la mano," Op. 2; Variations on a German Air*)

SONATA FOR PIANO No. 2,
IN B-FLAT MINOR, OP. 35
(*Composed in 1839*)

The impact that the B-flat minor Sonata had

upon the contemporary scene can be gauged from Schumann's review. Even Schumann, who so admired Chopin and was so familiar with his idiom, found it puzzling. "Any one," he wrote, "who could glance at the first bars of the [B-flat minor] Sonata, and then remain in uncertainty as to who had written it, would not prove himself a good connoisseur. Only Chopin begins and ends so: with dissonances through dissonances into dissonances. But how many beauties, too, this piece contains! The idea of calling it a sonata is a caprice, if not a jest, for he has simply bound together four of his wildest children, to smuggle them under this name into a place to which they could not else have penetrated." Schumann mentioned the "often wild and arbitrary chords" in the sonata, and the finale really unhorsed him. It sounded to Schumann "more like a joke than a piece of music. Yet we must confess that even from this joyless, unmelodious movement, an original, a terrible mind breathes forth, the preponderance of which annihilates resistance, so that we listen, fascinated and uncomplaining, to the end; but not to praise; for, as I have said before, this is not music. The sonata commences enigmatically, and closes with an ironic smile, a sphinx." But it is a measure of Schumann the man and Schumann the critic, that he was able to write: "Chopin no longer writes anything that we could have equally good from others; he is true to himself, and has good reasons for remaining so." The finale, which so bothered Schumann, is a short, fast piece in unison notes that is marked *sotto voce* and disappears before it starts. "The Wind Over the Grave," impressionable Victorian critics were wont to call it.

The Rachmaninoff re-pressing is something all collectors of Chopin and great piano playing should have. What a buy! Two of the most important piano works of the nineteenth century (Schumann's *Carnaval* is included), played by a titanic pianist of a previous generation, in LP transfers that retain much of the original quality —and all for $1.98. Rachmaninoff recorded the Chopin sonata on February 18, 1930. It is a staggering and literally inimitable performance. Rachmaninoff was trained around the turn of the century, when pianists and public were not as purist-minded as they are today. It was expected that the artist should enjoy considerable leeway, even to the point of reinforcing specific passages for greater technical effect. Rachmaninoff, himself a composer, was less apt than many of his colleagues to alter the music, but he did touch up passages here and there. There are sections in the B-flat minor Sonata that are downright arbitrary. Yet by the force of his conception and the consistency of his musical approach, Rachmaninoff makes the sonata a tremendous experience. He plays the third movement, the "funeral march," as Anton Rubinstein was supposed to have played it: starting pianissimo, building to a ferocious climax up to the trio, resuming the fortissimo at the end of the trio, and then tapering to a pianissimo at the end. The idea is that of a procession coming from a distance and then receding into the distance. Apart from this, there are many details in the sonata that leave one gasping. Not the least of these is the miraculous ease with which Rachmaninoff negotiates the tricky figurations in the outer parts of the scherzo.

The Novaes performance is beautiful. She has the three T's—Technique, Tone, and Temperament. In the enigmatic last movement she finds things in the way of inner voices that I have not heard since Hofmann was in his prime. Altogether a superb achievement. Rubinstein's forceful statement of the music is also worth owning, though the recorded sound shows its age. Both of the Gilels performances are a little puzzling. He has a singing tone and a big style, but he seems afraid to let himself go, and the interpretations sound inhibited. Very clear playing here, but uncommunicative. Brailowsky is accurate, experienced and, like Gilels, uncommunicative. Janis just misses the top. He may not be possessed of a blazing temperament, but he has taste, excellent coordination and first-class technical equipment. He plays in a manner unusually faithful to the notes, and also to the rhythmic scheme. If, with all this, his playing had a little more urgency and personality, a little more imagination and color, he could make some of his more highly touted colleagues run for cover. None of the other performances of the B-flat minor Sonata is outstanding. Katchen goes through the notes in brilliant fashion, but the playing is all on the surface. The Casadesus performance I find neat, polite and small-scaled. Uninsky plays the notes and little more. Horowitz strives for big effects but merely manages to sound petulant. This is one of his least successful records. Backhaus is miscast here, and he misses the passion of the music. His Teutonic muse strokes a heavy lyre. Malcuzynski I find incomprehensible. If this is good Chopin playing, then the great exponents of the past, like Rachmaninoff, Hofmann, Lhevinne and Rosenthal were on the wrong track. I find this playing spasmodic and actually unsettling.

——Sergei Rachmaninoff. RCA CAMDEN 396 (with Schumann: *Carnaval*)

——Guiomar Novaes. Vox PL 7360 (with *Sonata No. 3, in B minor, Op. 58*)

——Artur Rubinstein. RCA VICTOR LVT 1042 (with **Debussy**: Piano music)   NOTE: This disc was originally released as 78-rpm set 1082, and then transferred to LP as LM 9008.

——Byron Janis. RCA Victor LM 2091 (with *Impromptu No. 1, in A-flat, Op. 29; Nocturne No. 8, in D-flat, Op. 27, No. 2; "Black Key" Étude No. 5, in G-flat, Op. 10, No. 5; Mazurka No. 45, in A minor, Op. 67, No. 4; Scherzo No. 3, in C-sharp minor, Op. 39*)

——Emil Gilels. Angel 35308 (with Shostakovich: *Three Preludes and Fugues: Nos. 24, in D minor; 1, in C; and 5, in D*)

——Emil Gilels. Colosseum 256 (with music by Scarlatti, etc.)

——Alexander Brailowsky. RCA Victor LM 1866 (with *Sonata No. 3, in B minor, Op. 58*)

——Vladimir Horowitz. RCA Victor LM 1235 (with *Ballade No. 1, in G minor, Op. 23; Nocturne No. 5, in F-sharp, Op. 15, No. 2*; Liszt: *Au bord d'une source; Hungarian Rhapsody No. 6*)

——Robert Casadesus. Columbia ML 4798 (with *4 Ballades*)

——Alexander Uninsky. Epic LC 3056 (with *Sonata No. 3, in B minor, Op. 58*)

——Wilhelm Backhaus. London LLP 266 (with Beethoven: *Sonata No. 30, in E, Op. 109*)

——Julius Katchen. London LL 1163 (with *Sonata No. 3, in B minor, Op. 58*)

——Witold Malcuzynski. Angel 35032 (with *Sonata No. 3, in B minor, Op. 58*)

SONATA FOR PIANO NO. 3, IN B MINOR, OP. 58
(*Composed in 1844*)

This is a concert-hall perennial. Fairly long,
difficult, effective, it has attracted virtuoso
pianists since 1844. The third movement is hard
to sustain. It is slow and dreamlike, with a few
curious anticipations of Debussy, and in inex-
perienced hands it falls apart. In the last movement, Chopin is at his most glittering. It is the
most objective of the four movements, and it
immediately announces its intentions with the
mighty upward octave swoops. Three admirable
LP versions are on the market. Novaes makes
the most personal experience of the music, taking, in all truth, a good many liberties. But she
has the genius to make her own rules, and everything she does sounds right—for her. Imitators
would come to grief. Kapell here is represented
by what I think is the greatest disc he made. This
is a perfectly proportioned reading, brilliantly
executed, sharply defined. What a master he
would have developed into! Lipatti is the most
sober of the trio. He plays the music "straight,"
with taste and polished execution. I find it a
shade noncommittal and lacking in inner glow.
The music would have grown on him had he
lived. Nevertheless a magnificent achievement;
and it is only because the pianist is Lipatti that
one automatically measures his disc against the
highest of standards. The recording, British

Columbia vintage 1947, lacks clarity and has a heavy bass. Brailowsky is at his best in his recording, playing accurately and, frequently, powerfully. What is lacking is personality. Uninsky is disappointing. He does not seem to be able to bring the music to life. Everything is correct; nothing happens. Of the Malcuzynski and Katchen versions, see the remarks in the discussion of the B-flat minor Sonata.

A few remarks about the Rosenthal disc are in order. Rosenthal was the last active exponent of the Liszt school. When he died, in 1946, only José Viana da Motta, a Portuguese pianist who had been inactive as a recitalist for some years, remained. (Da Motta died two years after Rosenthal.) Rosenthal did make quite a few recordings that appeared during his lifetime, but on this disc Camden has come up with items that were never released. The B minor Sonata was recorded in 1939, at which time he was seventy-seven years old. In his prime he was known as one of the great thunderers; the pianist with the most heroic of styles and most stupendous of techniques. In his old age he no longer had the strength to storm through the music and had to substitute finesse. His fingers no longer obeyed him, and there is some fumbling. But what craft and style are here!—and what variety of touch!—and what a singing tone! This quality of tone, luscious, velvety and never percussive, is found in all the great turn-of-the-century pianists, who knew how to coax from the instrument a type of coloration that seems to be entirely alien to today's younger generation. And thus, despite inaccuracies of a technical nature, this disc is in truth a document. It represents not only Moriz Rosenthal but also a certain era and philosophy of the keyboard. The recorded sound is as good as can be expected. There is one bad tape splice, at bar 143 of the last movement, which obviously was intended as a 78-rpm turnover point.

——Guiomar Novaes. Vox PL 7360 (with *Sonata No. 2, in B-flat minor, Op. 35*)

——William Kapell. RCA Victor LM 1715 (with *9 Mazurkas*)

——Dinu Lipatti. Columbia ML 4721 (with *Barcarolle, Op. 60; Nocturne No. 8, in D-flat, Op. 27, No. 2; Mazurka No. 32, in C-sharp minor, Op. 50, No. 3*)

——Moriz Rosenthal. RCA Camden 377 (with *Tarantelle, Op. 43;* pieces by Chopin-Liszt, Handel, and Strauss-Rosenthal)

——Alexander Brailowsky. RCA Victor LM 1866 (with *Sonata No. 2, in B-flat minor, Op. 35*)

——Alexander Uninsky. Epic LC 3056 (with *Sonata No. 2, in B-flat minor, Op. 35*)

——Julius Katchen. London LL 1163 (with *Sonata No. 2, in B-flat minor, Op. 35*)

——Witold Malcuzynski. Angel 35032 (with *Sonata No. 2, in B-flat minor, Op. 35*)

TARANTELLE, IN A-FLAT, OP. 43
(*Composed in 1841*)

A rather charming work, minor Chopin. The composer had Rossini's famous tarantelle, *La Danza*, in mind. In a letter to a friend, he inquired if Rossini's tarantelle was in six-eight or twelve-eight time. "People write it both ways, but I should like mine to be the way Rossini has it." Schumann was impressed. "This is in Chopin's most daring manner," he wrote. "We see the madly whirling dancers before us until our own senses seem to reel." There are two competent modern performances. Banhalmi is clear and spirited; Mauro-Cottone is lighter but more stylish. Of the others, the veteran Rosenthal is severely taxed technically, though his tone still is capable of nuance. Entremont is surprisingly heavy-sounding. Balogh takes a tempo that is on the slow side, and some of his attack sounds flurried.

——George Banhalmi. Vox PL 10370 (with *Variations on a German Air; Nocturne in C-sharp minor, posth.; Prelude in A-flat, posth.; Prelude in C-sharp minor, Op. 45; Rondo in E-flat, Op. 16; Barcarolle, Op. 60; Bolero, Op. 19; Variations Brillantes, Op. 12*)

——Aurora Mauro-Cottone. KAPP 9012 (with encore pieces)

——Moriz Rosenthal. RCA CAMDEN 377 (with *Sonata No. 3, in B minor, Op. 58*; pieces by Chopin-Liszt, Handel, and Strauss-Rosenthal)

——Philippe Entremont. EPIC LC 3316 (with *Nocturne No. 8, in D-flat, Op. 27, No. 2; Impromptu No. 1, in A-flat, Op. 29; Scherzo No. 1, in B minor, Op. 20; Polonaises: Nos. 5, in F-sharp minor, Op. 44; and 3, in A, Op. 40, No. 1; Ballade No. 3, in A-flat, Op. 47*)

——Erno Balogh. LYRICHORD LL 20 (with *4 Impromptus; Bolero, Op. 19; Berceuse, Op. 57; Barcarolle, Op. 60*)

VARIATIONS BRILLANTES, OP. 12
(*Composed in 1833*)

Even Schumann did not think much of this set of variations. "It must be confessed that these variations ought not to be compared to his original works." A potboiler, this Op. 12 is the kind of fashionable potpourri that was so prevalent among the pianist-composers of the period. Chopin based his work on an aria named *Je vends des scapulaires* from Hérold's *Ludovic*. Hérold was a most successful opera composer in the early nineteenth century. Only his *Zampa* Overture survives. About all a pianist can do with the *Variations Brillantes* is play with a flexible technique and all the elegance at his disposal. Banhalmi has the technique, though his elegance is rather in short order. His performance, however, is better than Goldsand's, who plays neatly but with a singular lack of tension. Granted that the music is no heavyweight, it still demands more than an indifferent run-through.

——George Banhalmi. Vox PL 10370 (with *Variations on a German Air; Tarantelle, Op. 43; Nocturne in C-sharp minor, posth.; Rondo in E-flat, Op. 16; Prelude in A-flat, posth.; Prelude in C-sharp minor, Op. 45; Barcarolle, Op. 60; Bolero, Op. 19*)

——Robert Goldsand. CONCERT HALL H 1633 (with *Études, Op. 25*). NOTE: This disc was originally issued as CHS 1133.

VARIATIONS ON "LÀ CI DAREM LA MANO," OP. 2 (*Composed in 1827*)

The "*Là ci darem la mano*" Variations were originally scored for piano and orchestra. The work has been recorded in that form by Orazio Frugoni and the Pro Musica Orchestra under Hans Swarowsky (see above). As in the case of the similarly scored Andante Spianato and Polonaise, the "*Là ci darem*" Variations can be played as a piano solo (though the former work is a concert-hall staple, whereas the variations are almost never heard). Only two versions are available—the above-mentioned Frugoni, for piano and orchestra, and the Goldsand, for solo piano. Goldsand's version is preferable. He gets more nuance and flexibility into his playing, and he has a greater understanding of the idiom. He does take a rather sizable cut in the introduction (Frugoni is complete), and that is a mark against his disc, but otherwise his performance is that of a sensitive musician and a brilliant technician.

——Robert Goldsand. CONCERT HALL H 1650 (with *Variations on a German Air; Sonata No. 1, in C minor, Op. 4*) NOTE: This disc was originally released as CHS 1150.)

VARIATIONS ON A GERMAN AIR
(*Composed in 1826*)

An example of juvenilia. Chopin was sixteen when he composed these variations, based on a song named *Der Schweizerbub* ("The Swiss Boy"), a naïve melody with yodel-like characteristics. No opus number attaches to this youthful effort. Goldsand plays conscientiously and simply; Banhalmi, ditto. Anybody interested in the music can select either interpretation with confidence.

——George Banhalmi. Vox PL 10370 (with *Tarantelle, Op. 43; Nocturne in C-sharp minor, posth.; Rondo in E-flat, Op. 16; Prelude in A-flat, posth.; Prelude in C-sharp minor, Op. 45; Barcarolle, Op. 60; Variations Brillantes, Op. 12; Bolero, Op. 19*)

——Robert Goldsand. CONCERT HALL H 1650 (with *Sonata No. 1, in C minor, Op. 4; Variations on "Là ci darem la mano," Op. 2*) NOTE: This disc was originally released as CHS 1150.

VARIATIONS ON AN AIR BY HÉROLD
See Variations Brillantes, Op. 12

WALTZES (COMPLETE)
(*Most editions contain fourteen waltzes. Opus*

*numbers and dates of composition are as follows:
Op. 18, composed in 1831; Op. 34, Nos. 1-3,
composed in 1835, 1831 and 1838; Op. 42, 1840;
Op. 64, Nos. 1-3, 1846-47; Op. 69, Nos. 1-2,
1835 and 1829; Op. 70, Nos. 1-3, 1835, 1843 and
1829; Waltz in E minor, 1830; Waltz in E, 1829.
The latter two are without opus numbers, and
the E major is not contained in many editions of
the waltzes.)*

Considering the popularity of the waltzes, it is
surprising how few pianists have recorded complete versions. Fortunately Rubinstein has taken
care of the situation, playing in a free manner
that yet never loses sight of the fact that the
waltz is a dance form with a clearly defined
meter. A typically beautiful Rubinstein performance. Novaes achieves a swinging, gracious
quality, using plenty of rubato, sounding entirely
relaxed, bringing a highly personal quality to
her playing. Lipatti, in his Columbia disc, is much
more strict. He takes very few liberties, and
while his interpretations are to be admired for
their clarity and straightforward rhythm, he does
not fully capture the spontaneity of the music.
His Angel album is a poignant souvenir of his
art. It was recorded at his last public performance, at the Besançon Festival in 1950. Lipatti
was near death at the time, and he was so weak
that he had to be drugged before going on stage.
Nobody would guess his physical condition from

these poised, beautiful performances. Only in the
ending of the A-flat (Op. 42) Waltz is there an
apparent weakening. None of the other LP versions has much to offer. Brailowsky and Pennario are stiff and uninteresting, and both hit the
piano in a percussive manner. Doyen plays carefully, accurately and coldly. His rhythms are too
regular, his dynamics tend toward monotony,
and in general the playing sounds depersonalized.
——Artur Rubinstein. VICTOR LM 1892
——Guiomar Novaes. VOX PL 8170
——Dinu Lipatti. ANGEL 35439 NOTE: This performance of the waltzes is also contained in the
entire Besançon recital, ANGEL 3556B, 2 discs,
with Bach: *Partita No. 1, in B-flat;* Mozart:
Sonata No. 8, in A minor, K. 310; Schubert: *Impromptus in E-flat and G-flat, Op. 90, Nos. 2 and
3*).
——Dinu Lipatti. COLUMBIA ML 4522
——Jean Doyen. EPIC LC 3468
——Alexander Brailowsky. RCA VICTOR LM
1082
——Leonard Pennario. CAPITOL P 8172

WALTZES (INDIVIDUAL)

An alphabetical look at some pianists who have
recorded Chopin waltzes would begin with
Backhaus, who on LONDON LL 1556 (Chopin
recital) offers a surprisingly jaunty performance
of the Waltz No. 2, in A-flat, Op. 34, No. 1. Cor
de Groot has a *Minute Waltz*—the Waltz No. 6,

in D-flat, Op. 64, No. 1—soberly played on Epic LC 3037 (Chopin recital), along with the popular Waltz No. 7, in C-sharp minor, Op. 64, No. 2. Entremont, in his Chopin recital (Concert Hall CHS 1502), plays the *Minute;* C-sharp minor; No. 3, in A minor, Op. 34, No. 2; No. 5, in A minor, Op. 42; No. 9, in A-flat, Op. 69, No. 2; and 13, in D-flat, Op. 70, No. 3, and handles the music with plenty of character and sophistication. A fine disc, though unfortunately the recorded sound is inferior. From Firkusny, on Capitol PAO 8428 (Chopin recital), comes No. 1, in E-flat, Op. 18, and also the C-sharp minor, both elegantly played. Hofmann's delicious performance of the *Minute Waltz* is contained in Columbia ML 4929. Horowitz has No. 3 in A minor and the C-sharp minor in RCA Victor LM 1137 (Chopin recital). He plays both waltzes in a severely lyric manner, determined to avoid any allegation of excess virtuosity. On Angel 35171 (Chopin recital), Malcuzynski plays the *Minute* and No. 11, in G-flat, Op. 70, No. 1; and on Angel 35348 (recital) he can be heard in the C-sharp minor and No. 14, in E minor. These are routine performances. Nadas has a well-articulated *Minute Waltz* on Period 722 (Chopin recital), and Novaes a lovely C-sharp minor on Vox PL 7810 (Chopin recital). Still another C-sharp minor, and a most dignified one, comes from Paderewski on RCA Camden 310 (recital).

Chamber Music

INTRODUCTION AND POLONAISE BRILLANTE,
FOR CELLO AND PIANO, OP. 3
(*Composed in 1829*)

Chopin himself had no large opinion of his agreeable but essentially superficial *Introduction and
Polonaise Brillante*. He had composed it for a
Viennese cellist named Joseph Merk, and in a
letter to a friend he admitted that "there is
nothing in it but glitter—a salon piece for ladies."
Rostropovich plays the work with a rich tone
and secure intonation. He is accompanied by a
very brilliant pianist. The piano part is as important as the cello part in this work; indeed, it
is more interesting, and demands an artist of
unusual accomplishments.
——Mstislav Rostropovich, cello; Alexander
Dedyukhin, piano. WESTMINSTER XWN 18688
(with encore pieces by Granados, Prokofieff,
etc.)

SONATA FOR CELLO AND PIANO, IN G MINOR,
OP. 65
(*Composed in 1845-46*)

One of Chopin's best friends was the French cellist Auguste-Joseph Franchomme, and it is to him that the composer dedicated the work, one of his last compositions. For some reason this fine score is seldom played in concert, and there is only one LP recording (though prior versions by Kurtz and Piatigorsky have been discontinued). It is exceptionally rich harmonically, and it has some lovely melodic content. The opening vaguely recalls the E minor Concerto. During the course of the second movement, a D major theme of unusual warmth occurs; one would have thought that such a lovely lyric idea alone would have insured the success of the sonata; and this is not the only lyric inspiration. The poignant theme that starts the third movement is another. In the finale the listener is once more in the world of the piano concertos, with a strongly national theme put through florid paces. The only LP recording is not too satisfactory. Parisot is lyric but small-scaled, with intonation not always dead-centered and with a lack of tension in shaping the musical lines. A stronger performance is badly needed.

——Aldo Parisot, cello; Leopold Mittman, piano. OVERTONE 17 (with Mendelssohn: *Variations Concertantes, Op. 17;* Schubert: *Arpeggione Sonata*)

TRIO FOR PIANO AND STRINGS,
IN G MINOR, OP. 8
(*Composed 1828-29*)

Again we probably owe the G minor Trio to the
urgings of Joseph Xavier Elsner, Chopin's
teacher. Elsner tried to get Chopin to write
"classic" works; and what could be more classic
than a trio? The work is a youthful effort, but
it has some interesting points. In effect it is a
baby piano concerto, with the piano getting the
lion's share of the work. The last movement, in
Chopin's nationalistic vein, is quite charming.
Schumann was fond of it. In his review, he re-
minded his public that he, Robert Schumann, had
been the first to introduce Chopin. "And how
finely Chopin has realized his prophecy, how
triumphantly he has issued from the fight with
the ignoramuses and Philistines, how nobly he
still strives onward, ever more simply and artis-
tically! Even this trio belongs to Chopin's earlier
works, when he still gave the preference to the
virtuoso. . . . Is it not as noble as possible, more
enthusiastic than the song of any poet, original
in detail as in the whole, every note life and
music?" Extravagant words for an unimportant
(over a hundred years removed, we have second
sight) Chopin work. But then we pause to think
over Schumann's words. He was a sensitive critic
and a great musician. Would a piece of second-

rate material have so excited him? No; and the conclusion is inescapable. Even minor Chopin hit the Eighteen-Thirties with a force that today cannot be realized. And, in fairness to Schumann, who were the composers whose trios he had to review? There were J. Rosenhain, Anton Bohrer, A. Hesse, F. W. Jähns, J. C. Louis Wolf, Ambroise Thomas (yes; he of *Mignon*)—but why continue? I have not heard the trios of Messrs. Rosenhain, Bohrer & Co., but it is a safe guess that Chopin's trio stood out among them like a battleship in a fishing fleet.

The only currently available LP recording comes from three eminent Russian musicians— David Oistrakh, Mstislav Rostropovich, and Lev Oborin. Each is an experienced chamber music player, and they combine to maximum effect. Oborin is an unusually fine pianist, and the difficulties of his part dissolve under his agile fingers. The quality of recorded sound is good. ——David Oistrakh, violin; Mstislav Rostropovich, cello; Lev Oborin, piano. WESTMINSTER XWN 18174 (with Ravel: *Trio*)

Songs

SEVENTEEN POLISH SONGS, OP. 74
(*Composed between 1829 and 1847*)

It is surprising that Chopin composed so little vocal music. He adored the singing voice, and in these highly nationalistic pieces he composed very unusual music. They are to the song literature what the mazurkas are to the world of piano music. Exotic, with modal turns of phrase and a permeating nostalgia, they are no mere translations of Polish tunes. The imprint of Chopin is upon them. The names of the seventeen songs are: 1. *Życzenie* (Desire); 2. *Wiosna* (Spring); 3. *Smutna Rzeka* (Sorrowful River); 4. *Hulanka* (Revelry); 5. *Gdzie lubi* (Where She Loves); 6. *Precz z moich oczu* (Away from My Eyes); 7. *Poseł* (Messenger); 8. *Sliczny chłopiec* (Handsome Lad); 9. *Melodya* (Melody); 10. *Wojak* (Warrior); 11. *Dwojacki Koniec* (Double Ending); 12. *Moja piesczotka* (My Sweetheart); 13. *Niema czego trzeba* (There Is No Reason Why It Must Be); 14. Pierścień (Ring); 15. *Narzeczony* (Bridegroom);

16. *Pionska litewska* (Little Lithuanian Song); and 17. *Spiew grobowy* (Sepulchral Song). Kurenko sings the songs in the original Polish, using her hard but clear voice with consistent artistry. She has received sparkling recorded sound.

——Maria Kurenko, soprano; Robert Hufstader, piano. LYRICHORD LL 23.

Robert Schumann

Born Zwickau, Germany, June 8, 1810; died Endenich, Germany, July 29, 1856

When Robert Schumann died in 1856, it was after a lifetime of struggle, misunderstanding and ceaseless work. It was not that he was completely neglected during his own day. No great composer ever has been; and, after all, among the hundreds of prominent musicians active in the 1830's, it was Schumann to whom the young Brahms turned for study and advice. Genius attracts genius. But whereas professionals and the avant-garde of Schumann's lifetime took a great interest in his music, most of the concert-goers and critics completely failed to respond to his romanticism, his compositional eccentricities and his intense introspection. Clara Wieck, his wife and one of the most popular pianists in Europe, never could put Schumann's keyboard music across during his lifetime. Even Liszt himself, the pianistic idol of the time, failed miserably with the *Carnaval* and wrote Schumann

apologetic letters for not programming his music.
(Liszt always knew which side his bread was
buttered on.) That great pompous ass, Henry
Fothergill Chorley—the most powerful critic in
England—apparently took Schumann's music as
a personal insult. In 1852 he wrote about what he
considered the characteristics of "Dr. Schumann's" music—"The same skill of covering
pages with thoughts little worth noting, and of
hiding an intrinsic poverty of invention, by
grim or monotonous eccentricity. There is a
style, it is true, in Dr. Schumann's music—a certain thickness, freaked with frivolity—a mastery
which produces no effect—a resolution to de-
ceive the ear, which (as in the case of certain
French composers)"—Chorley here is referring
to Berlioz—"ends in habituating the ear to the
language of deception; and spoils the taste without substituting any new sensations of pleasure."
Chorley then bewails the possible future date
when Schumann's music might be accepted by
the public. This, he believes, would imply a
decadence of taste even worse than that which
obtained in the miserable and heathenish days of
1848.

How wrong can a listener be? Even at the
removal of over a hundred years, and with Schumann safely established as a classic, it is difficult
to understand how a presumably qualified critic
around 1850 could fail to respond to *certain*

aspects of the music. Granted that some of the harmonies were harsh. Granted that some of the rhythmic suspensions, dislocations and syncopations (among Schumann's favorite devices) were inexplicable to ears not far removed from Mozart's. Granted that the form had little or nothing to do with classic form. But what about the individual melodic lines? And the dedicated personality that comes through everything Schumann wrote? And, above all, the feeling of sheer, unmistakable poetry?

For Schumann was among the most personal and poetic of composers. Of all the romantics, Chopin and Berlioz included, he was the most romantic, the one most symbolic of his age, the most introspective and the one most responsive to the new art form that were sweeping Europe. And he was also the most dedicated.

All great composers are, of course, dedicated men, but Schumann's passion was something special. He pursued a single course for his entire life, wrapped only in the mantle of music. He composed it, wrote about it, tried to teach and conduct it. He was a cultured, widely read man, but all of that culture and reading were channeled into music. It was not enough to read Byron; he had to compose a *Manfred*. He admired E. T. A. Hoffman's writings, and the result was a *Kreisleriana* and goodness knows how many other untitled pieces of music. Whatever he read, whatever he heard, whatever he did took on a musical significance for him.

His was a flame that burned eternally hot and finally engulfed him. Only Berlioz matched him in enthusiasm for the cause of romantic music, but Berlioz had neither Schumann's generosity nor scope; he was much more egocentric. Consider the other romantics. Mendelssohn (so beloved of Chorley) had great honesty but nowhere comparable vision. Chopin moved in his own orbit, completely uninterested in the work of his fellow romantics. Liszt flitted here and there, another egocentric, a genius who lacked focus and discipline, a generous spirit who gloried in his own generosity and the adulation of others.

To this day Schumann presents problems, though many of those problems are of an extra-musical nature. His music has in it many elements of autobiography—elements that meant much more to him than to any listener. From the very beginning Schumann was a flaming romantic. He was a little sentimental, as all ardent young men should be; perhaps a little over-anxious to coin a neat phrase and express exalted poetic sentiments. At the age of sixteen he imagined himself in love and delivered himself of the following sentiment: "O friend! were I but a smile, how I would flit about her eyes! were I but joy, how gently would I throb in her pulses! yea, might I be but a tear, I would weep with her, and then if she smiled again, how gladly would I die on her eyelash, and gladly, gladly, be no more!" It is known that he wanted to be a poet. Gravely he writes, as early as 1827, "My whole life revels now in the sweet flower-garden of Memory, where I pluck many a lovely 'Immortelle,' which, though faded, I press for ever to my sorrowing heart, and kiss the withered blossoms of a happy life. Neither have I a friend any longer, with whom to ramble through the flowery vales of Pindus." These Byronic young men! Did Schumann, in later life, pick up letters like this and blush?

We read in his early letters about his overpowering passion for Jean Paul, his preoccupation with Homer, Horace and the other classics, his developing musical tastes. At that time Schumann was a perfectly normal young man, with none of the melancholia that was to mar his later life. From Zwickau, on December 1, 1827, he writes to a friend, describing a drinking bout in which he took part—a bout that developed into a party in which the local rustics participated. "I danced with that gentle, modest Minchen of the Müllers . . . we rejoiced and rushed about, staggering among the legs of the clodhoppers, and then took a tender farewell of the whole company by imprinting smacking kisses on the lips of all the peasant girls."

Although Schumann, to please his mother, went to Leipzig to study law, he made no pretense at enjoying it. He was like a fish trying to get off a hook, at first gently tugging, finally making a hysterical dash that completely broke the legal line which was trying to reel him in. At the beginning he mildly remonstrated. "The study of law, which crushes one at the beginning by its cut-and-dried definitions, does not suit me at all." Fortunately he had a piano in his chambers, and spent much more time studying music than jurisprudence, though he never told his mother that. He also spent some time in fencing school—fancy Schumann the duelist!—smoked many cigars, and spent his evenings playing chess or going to concerts. He apologizes to his mother for the fencing "because it is absolutely necessary and even useful. But I have never been a fighting character, and never shall be, and you need not be alarmed about duels, though one has to be very careful." As, indeed, one had to be, in those days at a German university.

As time goes on, his letters to his mother, though honorably dutiful, become impatient and restless. Music was calling. To his musical friends he lets his hair down, and then we can see what this young scoundrel of a law student really was doing. "I have begun many a symphony," he writes Friedrich Wieck in 1829. Wieck was Schumann's only important teacher. Schumann had gone to Heidelberg not to study law (as he told his mother) but really to work on piano and composition in his teacher's home town. "Without overestimating my own abilities, I feel modestly conscious of my superiority over all the early Heidelberg pianists." There follows an enthusiastic eulogy of Schubert, who was still generally unknown. In time, his mother began to have an inkling of what was going on, and the budding musician hastened to play down his activities, telling her a little white lie: "To one of your questions I must give a mournful answer —I mean about my music and piano playing. Alas! mother, it is almost at an end. I play but rarely now, and very badly. The grand Genius of Sound is gently extinguishing his torch, and all that I have ever done in music seems like a beautiful dream which I can hardly believe has ever existed. And yet, believe me, *if ever I could have done any good in the world it would have been in music,* and I feel sure (without at all overrating my capabilities) that I have *creative* power." The italics are Schumann's.

Little by little, his repressed musical desires triumphed over his mother's wishes. The letters covering this period are too well-known to discuss in detail, interesting as they are. His mother was horrified but had to make the best of it, contenting herself with a few pessimistic aphorisms concerning rotten trees and ensuing rotten fruit. She must have known, too, that something was going on between her Robert and Clara Wieck, the daughter of Friedrich. We all know how that particular episode turned out—the most beautiful love affair in music, one of the most romantic in history.

Schumann and his Clara were constantly exchanging letters, and Schumann's to his beloved are all-revealing. They show his artistic development; they show him, despite his reserved nature, to have been perfectly conscious of his abilities and perfectly confident in them. "Even to myself"—this letter is dated April 13, 1838, a time when Schumann had already achieved his mature compositional style—"my music seems wonderfully intricate in spite of its simplicity. Its eloquence comes straight from the heart, and everyone is affected when I play before people." Later: "Don't be afraid, my dear Clara, you shall live to see my compositions come into notice and be much talked about." He would go into detailed self-analysis: "In my latest compositions I often hear many things that I can hardly explain. It is most extraordinary how I write almost everything in canon, and then only detect the imitations afterwards, and often find inversions, rhythms in contrary motion, etc. I am paying great attention to melody now, as you may have found out. Much can be done on this point by industry and observation. But of course by 'melody' I mean something different from Italian aria, which always seem to me like the songs of birds—pretty to listen to, but without any depth of meaning."

Even more significant is the following passage, which in many respects is a clue to almost all of Schumann's music: "I am affected by everything that goes on in the world, and think it all over in my own way, politics, literature, and people, and then I long to express my feelings and find an outlet for them in music. That is why my compositions are sometimes difficult to understand, because they are connected with distant interests; and sometimes striking, because everything that happens impresses me, and compels me to express it in music. And that is why so few [modern] compositions satisfy me, because apart from all their faults of construction, they deal in musical sentiment of the lowest order, and in commonplace lyrical effusions. Theirs may be a flower, but mine is a poem; theirs is a mere natural impulse, mine the result of poetic consciousness. . . . And I cannot talk about it; in fact I can only speak of music in broken sentences, tho' I think a great deal about it. In short, you will find me very serious sometimes, and will not know what to make of me."

He writes to Clara about Mendelssohn, "certainly the most eminent man I have met." Schumann always had a great regard for Mendelssohn.

"I know exactly what he is to me in music, and could go on learning from him for years. But he can also learn something from me.—If I had grown up under the same circumstances as he did, and had been destined for music from childhood, I should now beat any one of you. I can feel that in the energy of my ideas."

No false modesty here. Poor Schumann had a right to be exasperated when he looked back over the "wasted" years of his childhood. And even more so when in his young manhood he had to waste his time on extracurricular matters when he should have been composing. Hence his explosion to Clara about her father, who never had a high opinion of Schumann's prospects. This on May 10, 1838. "Your father calls me phlegmatic! *Carnaval* and phlegmatic! F-sharp minor Sonata and phlegmatic! Being in love with such a girl and phlegmatic! And you can listen calmly to all this? He says that I have written nothing in the *Zeitung* for six weeks. In the first place that is not true. Secondly, even if it were, how does he know what other work I have been doing? . . . Up to the present time the *Zeitung* has had about eighty sheets of my own ideas, not to mention the rest of the editorial work, besides which I have finished ten major compositions in two years, and they have cost me some heart's blood. To add to all this, I have given several hours' hard study each day to Bach and Beethoven, and to my own work, and conscientiously managed a large correspondence, which was often very difficult and complicated. I am a young man of twenty-eight with a very active mind, and an artist to boot, yet for eight years I have not been out of Saxony. . . . And do you mean to say that all my industry and simplicity, and all that I have done, is quite lost upon your father?"

The portrait of the artist as a young man.

Schumann well knew himself. He is probably the most personal and introspective composer who ever lived. After he finished a piece of music, as he wrote to Clara above, he often found things in it that he had not realized in the process of composition. "I have just discovered that it strikes 12 at the end of the *Davidsbündlertänze*." This comes pretty close to unconscious writing. And it helps explain why complete understanding of his music is difficult. Any listener can, of course, enjoy the *Carnaval* for what it is, without inquiring into its *raison d'être*. But enjoyment and understanding are heightened when you come to realize that the music represents a kind of picture gallery in which are painted Schumann himself, Clara and Friedrich Wieck, Chopin, Mendelssohn, Paganini and others; and that the entire long composition is built on four notes (ASCH: S in German is our E-flat and H is our B natural) derived from the name of a town in which lived a lady-love of Schumann's. Can *Kreisleriana* really be understood without some knowledge of the strange career of E. T. A. Hoffmann? And these are titled pieces of music for which Schumann himself supplied the clue. In some other works, such as the Fantasy in C, the *Davidsbündlertänze* or the Symphonic Etudes, we can easily grasp the significance. But what about clueless works, such as the Intermezzi, Novelettes or F-sharp minor Sonata? Here we can only guess, building upon a knowledge of Schumann's style and symbolism.

He himself had come of middle-class parents. His father, a bookseller, had died when Robert was sixteen. Shortly before that, Robert's sister, a nineteen-year-old girl named Emilie, had committed suicide. There may have been a bad streak in the family line. And there certainly was nothing to account for the prodigy that Robert turned out to be. For despite the fact that he entered music professionally rather late in life, by the time he was sixteen he already was an expert pianist and a self-taught composer. His first aim, indeed, was to become a concert pianist, and he worked strenuously under Wieck to that end. But he was impatient and impetuous; and in an effort to hasten his piano technique, he invented a mechanism that was intended to strengthen the fingers. Instead he ruined his fourth finger, and thus disappeared all hopes for

a career as a piano virtuoso. Willy-nilly he became a composer (though, of course, he would
have become one in any event); and, in 1834,
he added to his chores the position of music
critic for the *Neue Zeitschrift für Musik*, a publication he helped found and for which he was
the first editor.

He was a great critic—able, honest, conscientious and ever ready to lend a helping hand to
new talent. Not much more than a generation
ago he was generally conceded to be the finest
music critic who ever lived. Then some doubters
came abroad, pointing out that he had hailed to
the skies such nonentities as Niels Gade and
Sterndale Bennett.

All of which, it seems to me, is completely unimportant. The question is not how many non-
enities he praised but how many geniuses he
failed to praise. The answer is hardly any. He
was one of the first to recognize the unique
qualities of Chopin, and he was the first to introduce Brahms. He had a little distrust of Berlioz,
but his criticism of the *Symphonie fantastique*
is fair, penetrating and extremely sensitive; and
he was big enough to say of it, "In spite of the
outward formlessness of this work, we must
recognize its intellectual coherence." He recognized Liszt for what he was, deploring the
"tinsel" in his music but hailing the advances in
piano technique and the harmonic innovations of

the Hungarian genius. Mendelssohn he adored. He was among the first to hail Schubert as a titan (he always had admired Schubert; and when he learned of Schubert's death, in 1828, he spent the whole night in tears). Beethoven and Bach were among his passions. Curiously, his only major lapse concerned a composer almost as revolutionary as he was—Richard Wagner. And yet he could say of *Tannhäuser:* "It is deep, original and a hundred times better than his earlier operas; and I consider the composition and instrumentation extraordinary, far beyond what he ever accomplished before." It must be remembered that Schumann died before hearing any of the great Wagner operas; and on the basis of what he did hear, he was not, perhaps, too wide of the mark.

Which is a pretty good record. It is even more impressive when one remembers that Schumann was a contemporary of most of these composers, and that none of them was then a "classic." And, far from being a perpetually genial writer, Schumann lashed out unmercifully at any kind of music he considered not up to the highest standards. He was the constant foe of Meyerbeerism and Rossini-ism. He disdainfully sneered at the manufactured-by-the-yard salon music of men like Herz and Hünten. Certainly he praised Gade. But Gade, when he came up, *was* a very promising talent. Schumann well recognized the dangers that were to beset the young man. He mentioned them in print, and it was not his fault if they all came true. As a prose stylist, Schumann may not have had the literary flair of a Berlioz or a Shaw; but if there ever was a greater music critic, the name does not come to mind.

For the most part, Schumann lived an uneventful life, the high point being the wooing and winning of Clara Wieck. There were nine years of age separating them. He was eighteen when he went to study with her father; she was nine. He saw her grow up, and their friendship ripened into passion. They became engaged in 1837, and her father promptly had everything but an apoplectic fit. It is easy to understand his point of view. Here he had carefully trained his prodigy of a daughter to the point where she was beginning to be recognized as one of the great pianists of Europe. (She was, incidentally, apparently the first, except for the composer himself, to play a work of Chopin's in public.) Was she then to throw herself away on a penniless composer with strange ideas? But while one can sympathize, old Wieck's actions took a course that has alienated him from any respect. He spread rumors about Schumann: that he was a drunkard, a misfit, an inferior composer; and he went so far as to disinherit his daughter. The couple had to take legal action for permission to marry without his consent. In 1840, the Court of Appeals decided in favor of the lovers, and they were married on September 12 of that year.

Up to that point Schumann had composed little but piano music. The year of their marriage he turned to the song, composing—incredibly— the contents of Op. 24 (*Liederkreis*), Op. 27, 29-31, 35, 36, 40, 42 (*Frauenliebe und Leben*), 45, 48 (*Dichterliebe*), 49 and 53. Even Schubert never worked so furiously over so brief a span; and these opus numbers of Schumann contain many masterpieces of the song literature. Then Schumann turned to symphonic writing and chamber music, though he never really stopped writing songs.

In 1843 he became professor of composition at the Leipzig Conservatory. Overwork brought him to a nervous breakdown the following year, and he had to give up the editorship of the *Neue Zeitschrift*. Nevertheless he continued to compose steadily, though he was suffering from a nervous attack, the precursor of the mental afflic- tion to which he eventually was to surrender. In an effort to seek a more favorable locale, he, Clara and the family (they had two children then and three were to follow) moved to Dres- den. His physician, a Dr. Helbig, ordered Schu- mann to get away from music for a while. As well order the sun to stop shining. "He first chose natural history," reported Dr. Helbig, "then natural philosophy, but abandoned them after a few days and gave himself up, wherever he might be, to his musical thoughts." In Dresden he conducted a choral society. Then, in 1849, he moved to Düsseldorf as conductor of the local symphony orchestra.

But this did not last too long. Temperamentally Schumann was not cut out to be a conductor. He had neither the dynamic personality nor the baton technique; and as he began to grow mentally more disturbed he began to live in a world of his own. Often he would continue beating time even though the orchestra was in a shambles. The absent-mindedness of the good Professor Schumann became a legend in Düsseldorf. Things finally came to a head. The directors of the orchestra politely—and reasonably enough, under the circumstances—asked him to refrain from conducting any but his own works: a face-saving device made in respect to Schumann's distinguished position in the world of music. Clara, who eternally protected her Robert, who loved him and was constantly trying to build up his ego, considered it an insult and was furious. She ended up getting the orchestra committee angry at her, and Schumann was fired. He never conducted again.

Darkness soon descended. There were auditory delusions, lapses in speech, melancholia. He thought angels were sending him themes and he wrote them down. In 1854 he tried to commit suicide by throwing himself into the Rhine River. Fishermen pulled him out. Nothing was left but to commit him, at his own request, to an asylum at Endenich, near Bonn. There he remained for the last two years, moments of lucidity alternating with complete release from the world. He died in the asylum on July 29, 1856. Clara wrote in her diary: "At 4 in the afternoon he fell peacefully asleep. His last hours were quiet and he passed away in his sleep without its being noticed; no one was with him at the moment. I did not see him until half an hour later. . . . His head was beautiful, the forehead so transparent and slightly arched. I stood by the body of my passionately loved husband and was calm. . . ."

During his lifetime he was the least popular of the great romantics. Not even Clara, so popular with concert audiences, could make his A minor Piano Concerto palatable at its Viennese première. "Calm yourself, dear Clara," said Schumann. "In ten years' time all this will have changed." (It took just about that. In 1860, old Moscheles was writing: "Only Beethoven's, Mendelssohn's, Schumann's and Chopin's concertos are now the fashion.") It never once occurred to Schumann that he could have had a great success by lowering his standards a little. He was a melodist with the best of them, and he could have turned out all the pretty, salable items that a publisher could have desired. Or he could have written cheap but temporarily effective *pièces d'occasion*, as Beethoven was not too proud to do in such works as *Wellington's Victory*. Not Schumann. When it came to art, he was the most uncompromising of idealists. How sad and wistful is one of his remarks to Clara!—"I confess it would be a great delight to me if I ever succeeded in writing something which, when played by you, would make the public dance with delight, for we composers are all of us vain, even when we have no reason to be so." Such successes were few in his lifetime.

His weaknesses as a composer have been thoroughly discussed—his discomfort with large forms, his deficiencies as an orchestrator, his occasional redundencies, the falling-off of inspiration in his last works. But in nearly everything he wrote—even in his unsuccessful pieces —there is a flaming imagination that lifts his music into a unique sphere of genius. Wrote he, in one of his aphorisms: "Thou must invent new and bold melodies." Schumann did invent new and bold melodies and harmonies.

Today, a little over a hundred years after his death, we find it difficult to realize just how revolutionary his music must have sounded. His music is the essence of romanticism. A strong classical element can be traced in Chopin, and Mendelssohn was a classicist more often than not. In Schumann there is virtually no classical current, although he knew the classicists as well as any man alive at the time, was a thorough student of counterpoint and, as he said, even *thought* polyphonically; and in this he stands alone among the German composers of the 1830's and 1840's. Now, our own century tends to be anti-romantic, and hence many listeners and professional musicians have experienced difficulty in achieving an identification with Schumann. So personal a composer is apt to provoke a violent personal reaction, pro or con. Some people find Schumann actually embarrassing. Others find him turgid and sentimental. Still others, this writer among them, regard him with perpetual love, admiration and delight. In his selfless absorption in music and in his defiant challenge to the Philistines, Schumann is as much a symbol as an individual. He never condescended and he catered to no audience. He desperately wanted success and fame, but on his own terms and according to his own principles; and his age did not meet those terms. His life was lived without concession or compromise. It was the life of a very great man.

Concertos

CONCERTO FOR CELLO AND ORCHESTRA, IN A MINOR, OP. 129
(*Composed in 1850*)

A mournful quality pervades this concerto, which is predominantly in the minor key, and even the major sections of the extraordinarily lyric slow movement (although the concerto is in one long movement, it has well-defined areas corresponding to "movements") have a feeling of the minor tonality. It takes a great cellist to convey the lyricism of the music. Much of the solo writing is ungrateful, with emphasis on the lower strings, and too many instrumentalists find themselves groaning along without relief. Of those who have recorded the work, Gendron achieves most success. His immense tone never loses quality, his phrasing has an altogether patrician elegance, and his left hand seems to be infallible. Of his generation of cellists, only Starker has this exactitude of pitch. But Starker seems, for some reason, to be a little uncomfortable in his recording of the Schumann. His playing, beautiful though it is, sounds a little episodic, and he does not have the conviction he displays in his other recordings. Utterly accomplished finger and bow work mark Starker's performance, however. The Fournier disc is excellent. This French cellist comes close to approximating the essential style. His interpretation, true, is rather tricky—full of unexpected nuances, reverse accents, and a great deal of vibrato. But a romantic outlook pervades his work and, in the slow movement, a really aristocratic conception that enables one to forget the mannerisms that crop up elsewhere. On hearing the Casals performance, on the other hand, one is first conscious of mannerism. This Casals disc has been a great puzzlement to his admirers. It comes close to being anarchistic: no basic tempo is maintained, the phrasings are entirely unorthodox, the intonation not always dead-center. The conductor, unnamed on the disc, is Eugene Ormandy.

Shafran's performance is interesting. The young (b. 1923) Russian gives the concerto an extremely virtuoso and not very subtle reading. He has a big style reminiscent of the early Piatigorsky, colorful tonal characteristics, and a vibrato that throbs just this side of vulgarity. Rostropovich's approach is altogether different, stressing the lyric elements of the score and sometimes becoming downright sentimental about them. Much of the playing is sensitive, but there are too many moments that lag, and the tempo of the slow movement is impossibly slow. Shuster's performance is able, but his tone is thin and unresonant. Fine musicianship here, but not always the most sensuous listening. Cassado fights too hard, not always successfully. His technique is not up to all demands, and his pitch often has a tendency to wander.

——Maurice Gendron; Orchestre de la Suisse Romande, Ernest Ansermet, cond. LONDON LL 947 (with Tchaikovsky: *Variations on a Rococo Theme*)

——Janos Starker; Philharmonia Orchestra, Carlo Giulini, cond. ANGEL 35598 (with Saint-Saëns: *Concerto for Cello and Orchestra in A minor, Op. 33*)

——Pierre Fournier; Philharmonia Orchestra, Sir Malcolm Sargent, cond. ANGEL 35397 (with Tchaikovsky: *Variations on a Rococo Theme*)

——Daniel Shafran; State Orchestra of the U.S.S.R., Kiril Kondrashin, cond. VANGUARD VRS 6028 (with Haydn-Piatigorsky: *Divertimento;* De Falla-Maréchal: *Suite populaire espagnole*)

——Mstislav Rostropovich; Moscow Philharmonic Orchestra, Samuel Samosud, cond. MONITOR MC 2023 (with *Concertstück for Four Horns and Orchestra, in F, Op. 86*).

——Joseph Schuster; Los Angeles Orchestral Society, Franz Waxman, cond. CAPITOL P 8232

(with Bruch: *Kol Nidrei;* J. C. Bach: *Concerto for Cello and Orchestra in C minor*)

——Gaspar Cassado; Bamberg Symphony, Jonel Perlea, cond. Vox PL 10210 (with Schubert-Cassado: *Concerto for Cello and Orchestra in C minor*)

——Pablo Casals; Prades Festival Orchestra, Eugene Ormandy, cond. COLUMBIA ML 4926 (with encore pieces).

CONCERTSTÜCK FOR FOUR HORNS
AND ORCHESTRA, IN F, OP. 86
(*Composed in 1849*)

Offhand, one would say that this is one of the most impractical scores ever written. How many performances could Schumann have expected with such a combination of solo instruments and orchestra? As it turned out, practically none. Certainly America has not heard the work for many years. It is a rather rambling piece, full of striking ideas that are never exploited as they should be. The four Russian horn virtuosos turn in an extremely competent performance, and Gauk supports them with full knowledge of what they are about.

——Y. Shapiro, B. Afanasiev, E. Stardzhilov, S. Krivnetsky, French horns; State Radio Orchestra of the U.S.S.R., Alexander Gauk, cond. MONITOR MC 2023 (*Concerto for Cello and Orchestra, in A minor, Op. 129*)

CONCERTO FOR PIANO AND ORCHESTRA,
IN A MINOR, OP. 54
(*Composed in 1845*)

No orchestral work of Schumann's needs less description. The Piano Concerto is one of his most popular pieces—eternally youthful and romantic. Of all the concertos in the repertoire, is there one with less virtuosity *per se?* I doubt it. Even Mozart intended most of his concertos as a vehicle for a great piano virtuoso, namely, W. A. Mozart. And, quite clearly, Brahms' two "symphonies for piano and orchestra" have the virtuoso pianist in mind. But not the gentle Schumann concerto. If one may digress for a moment, one of the features of Schumann's piano style is its uniform lack of showy virtuoso work coupled, paradoxically, to extreme technical difficulty. Schumann was not the natural pianist that Chopin and Liszt were. Nearly everything they wrote lies gratefully for the pianist's hand, whereas Schumann stubbornly went out of his way to throw complexities and problems into his writing. With him the musical, not the technical, idea was the thing; and if the musical idea meant a next-to-impossible figuration, so much the worse for the poor pianist. The Piano Concerto, however, is relatively straightforward in its writing, and it stays in the repertoire not because it is a virtuoso vehicle but because it is very beautiful music.

Several good performances are available. Perhaps the best, Lipatti's accurate and elegant interpretation, suffers from the most inferior sound, though it is of 1946 vintage and not impossible to enjoy. With a poised quality none of his competitors can match, Lipatti alone of all the pianists who have recorded the Schumann A minor keeps a steady, sure rhythmic pulse in the last movement. Serkin's disc has the richest recorded sound and contains his usual reliable, spirited playing touched by a slight nervous quality. Rubinstein's LP was originally released in 1948, as a 78-rpm album. His is not an economical buy, for Victor has spread the concerto over two sides. The recorded sound stands up well, however, and Rubinstein's red-blooded playing is, as always, a joy to hear. In the Novaes disc is encountered the freest playing, with an uncomfortably (and inexplicably) fast second movement, some very individual ideas throughout, and some light-fingered work that is sheer ravishment. (Vox has withdrawn Novaes' earlier recording of the concerto, with Klemperer and the Vienna Symphony.) The Haas recording is excellent—lyric, sensitive and unmannered. She is a most dependable pianist. The recorded sound is adequate but not very bright-sounding.

From here the curve takes a sharp drop.

Gulda's playing somewhat resembles Serkin's in its clear, direct attack, but he sounds more matter-of-fact. Furthermore the recording has a bass boom and a break between the second and third movements—a break that entirely ruptures the mood, for Schumann has linked the slow movement to the finale. Demus is prosaic and unimaginative. Haskil's disc has the dull tonal characteristics typical of early Epics, and the playing cannot be called much more than routine. Gieseking's disc was a disappointment. Neither technically nor tonally can it stand up to the good performances on LP. The Arrau performance is steady and reliable, with Arrau's wonderful fingers spinning out inhumanly even scales. But this disc has on the reverse side a distorted Grieg Piano Concerto (the Lipatti disc also has the Grieg concerto, magnificently played), which is enough to disqualify it. Tipo is strong rather than poetic, playing with very little charm. She quite misses the romanticism of the music. Bianca is tasteful but too small-scaled.

——Dinu Lipatti; Philharmonia Orchestra, Herbert von Karajan, cond. COLUMBIA ML 4525 (with Grieg: *Concerto for Piano and Orchestra, in A minor, Op. 16*) NOTE: The Schumann was previously issued on LP as 10-inch ML 2195.

——Rudolf Serkin; Philadelphia Orchestra, Eugene Ormandy, cond. COLUMBIA ML 5168 (with Strauss: *Burkeske for Piano and Orchestra*)

——Artur Rubinstein; NBC Symphony, William Steinberg, cond. RCA Victor LM 1050

——Guiomar Novaes; Pro Musica Orchestra of Vienna, Hans Swarowsky, cond. Vox PL 8540 (with *Kinderscenen*)

——Monique Haas; Berlin Philharmonic Orchestra, Eugene Jochum, cond. Decca DL 9868 (with Mozart: *Concerto for Piano and Orchestra in A, K. 488*)   Note: This performance was originally issued as 10-inch D 7522.

——Claudio Arrau; Philharmonia Orchestra, Alceo Galliera, cond. Angel 35561 (with Grieg: *Concerto for Piano and Orchestra, in A minor, Op. 16*)

——Friedrich Gulda; Vienna Philharmonic Orchestra, Volkman Andreae, cond. London LL 1589 (with Weber: *Concertstück*)

——Walter Gieseking; Philharmonia Orchestra, Herbert von Karajan, cond. Angel 35321 (with *Kinderscenen*)

——Clara Haskil; Hague Philharmonic Orchestra, Willem van Otterloo, cond. Epic LC 3020 (with Liszt: *Concerto for Piano and Orchestra No. 1, in E-flat*)

——Joerg Demus; Orchestra of the Vienna State Opera, Artur Rodzinski, cond. Westminster XWN 18290 (with *Introduction and Allegro, in D minor, Op. 134; Konzertstück, in G, Op. 92*); or XWN 18458 (with Chopin: *Concerto for Piano and Orchestra, in E minor, Op. 11*, played by Paul Badura-Skoda) Note: The Schumann was originally released as WL 5310.

——Maria Tipo; Pro Musica Orchestra of Vienna, Jonel Perlea, cond. Vox PL 10320 (with Chopin: *Concerto for Piano and Orchestra No. 2, in F minor, Op. 21*)

——Sondra Bianca; Philharmonia Orchestra of Hamburg, Arthur Winograd, cond. M-G-M E 3513 (with *Introduction and Allegro, in D minor, Op. 134; Konzertstück in G, Op. 92*)

CONCERTO FOR VIOLIN AND ORCHESTRA,
IN D MINOR
(Composed in 1853)

Although this record has been discontinued it is worth listing for the sake of completeness. It is the only version ever made of the Violin Concerto, a work now apparently out of the repertoire. There is a strange story behind the music. For many years the manuscript lay undisturbed. Then it was published in 1937 amid great hullabaloo, accompanied by séances at which Yelli d'Aranyi, who introduced the work, claimed to have been in contact with Schumann's ghost. But nothing helped the work itself. Menuhin included it in his repertoire for a while, and he even recorded it in the 1930's. Nobody today plays it—at least, it has not figured on a New York program for many years. It is one of Schumann's last works and not a very successful one, despite some brooding passages, occasional flashes of inspiration, and an unusual polonaise-like last movement. The strange slow movement is not very distinguished, yet somehow manages to be piercingly sad. One could wish for a more subtle violinist than Rybar, whose LP may now be hard to locate. His playing tends to be rough, and a general air of stolidity pervades the disc.

——Peter Rybar; Lausanne Festival Orchestra, Victor Desarzens, cond. CONCERT HALL CHS 1128.

Works for Solo Instrument and Orchestra

INTRODUCTION AND ALLEGRO FOR PIANO AND ORCHESTRA, IN D MINOR, OP. 134
(*Composed in 1853*)

Almost never heard, this is a vigorous and extremely Schumannesque work. The piano figurations are closely reminiscent of those in the Piano Concerto, and the broad melodies, while not as captivating as those in the Concerto, do grow on one. Demus presents a performance that is technically proficient and much more convincing than his versions of the Concerto and *Konzertstück* on the same disc. Bianca is not as well recorded as Demus, and her disc has considerable surface noise. She plays rather on the surface of the keys, prettily and ladylike but without much concentration.

——Joerg Demus, piano; Vienna State Opera Orchestra, Artur Rodzinski, cond. WESTMINSTER XWN 18290 (with *Concerto for Piano and Orchestra, in A minor, Op. 54; Konzertstück, in G, Op. 92*)

——Sondra Bianca, piano; Philharmonia State Orchestra of Hamburg, Arthur Winograd, cond. M-G-M E 3513 (with *Concerto for Piano and Orchestra, in A minor, Op. 54; Konzertstück, in G, Op. 92*)

KONZERTSTÜCK FOR PIANO AND ORCHESTRA, IN G, OP. 92
(*Composed in 1849*)

In 1950, a performance of this work by Erdmann and a Munich orchestra was released by Vox. That disc has been long withdrawn, leaving Demus and Bianca the sole exponents. The score also is known as the *Introduction and Allegro Appassionata*, and has been acclaimed by some admirers as top-notch Schumann. There are indeed some lovely sections in the score, including a Mendelssohnian opening *à la* the *Songs Without Words*. My edition of the music contains some Victorian descriptive prose that deserves reprint: "Composed in September 1849, the Concert Piece, without being able to vie with the Concerto Op. 54, in point of freshness of invention and brilliancy of execution, yet, by means of its poetic contents, its unity of mood, its clearness of form and clever thematic work, belongs among the prominent works of concert-literature and may with perfect justice claim, not merely for study, but also for its proper destination for public performance, the right of being rescued from unmerited oblivion." The allegro part of the music is energetically worked out in Schumann's best style, and it seems strange that pianists have neglected it. Serkin, several years ago, gave the only public performance New York has heard for many years, and one hopes he can be persuaded to record it. Demus here does no more than give a pedantic performance. The music is full of inner voices, specifically marked, that he simply does not observe. He plays the notes and that is all. The listener gets as much idea of the color of the piece as he would of a Renoir painting if he looked at it through sunglasses. Bianca is not any more convincing. She plays neatly, but it is all on the surface; nor is there, in her recording, the best balance between piano and orchestra.

——Joerg Demus, piano; Vienna State Opera Orchestra, Artur Rodzinski, cond. WESTMINSTER XWN 18290 (with *Concerto for Piano and Orchestra, in A minor, Op. 54; Introduction and Allegro for Piano and Orchestra, in D minor, Op. 134*)

——Sondra Bianca, piano; Philharmonia Orchestra of Hamburg, Arthur Winograd, cond. M-G-M E 3513 (with *Concerto for Piano and Orchestra, in A minor, Op. 54; Introduction and Allegro for Piano and Orchestra, in D minor, Op. 134*)

Orchestral Works

Braut von Messiana Overture, Op. 100
(Composed in 1851)

Scarcely a repertory item, the *Braut von Messiana* Overture probably has not received a performance in this country for years. It is a concert overture to the Schiller play and one of Schumann's few examples of rhetorical music. It is nowhere near the class of the powerful and imaginative *Manfred* Overture. On this disc it occupies the last third of side 2 of the Brahms A major Serenade. Winograd seems to feel the music and handles it with appropriate romanticism. Good recorded sound.

——Philharmonia Orchestra of Hamburg, Arthur Winograd, cond. M-G-M E 3437 (with Brahms: *Serenade No. 2, in A, Op. 16*)

Manfred Overture, Op. 115
(Composed in 1848)

For a discussion of the complete *Manfred*, see below, under Melodrama. Byron was one of Schumann's gods, and the *Manfred* Overture is

Schumann at his most Byronic, from the syncopated opening to the despairing sighs that close the work. No wonder the score is one of the composer's most successful orchestral pieces. It has everything—a rich harmonic scheme, warm melodies, and considerable rhythmic propulsion. Toscanini, in his recording, touches up the orchestration somewhat (he was not always the purist he was reputed to be). His is a violent, breathless interpretation with extraordinary drive, and against it all other versions tend to sound pallid. A noticeable "ghost," or pre-echo, disturbs the opening; otherwise the recorded sound is good. Kletzki tends toward sentimentalism (this is Byron with a poppy and a lily in his medieval hand), but he has by far the best recorded sound. The Lehmann disc features perfectly reliable orchestral playing and an energetic performance, perhaps a shade too fast. Münchinger's performance lacks personality, nor does his orchestra have the color of the competing ensembles.

——NBC Symphony, Arturo Toscanini, cond. RCA Victor LM 9022 (with Schubert: *Unfinished Symphony;* Beethoven: *Consecration of the House Overture*) Note: *Manfred* was originally issued as a 78-rpm album, and later on 10-inch LM 6.

——Israel Philharmonic Orchestra, Paul Kletzki, cond. Angel 35374 (with *Symphony No. 3*)

——Bamberg Symphony Orchestra, Fritz Leh-
mann, cond. DECCA DL 9905 (with Mendelssohn:
Calm Sea and Prosperous Journey; Schubert:
Rosamunde Overture; Magic Harp Overture;
Mendelssohn: *Fingal's Cave Overture*) NOTE:
Manfred was originally released on 10-inch DL
4017.

——Orchestre de la Suisse Romande, Karl
Münchinger, cond. LONDON LL 1551 (with
Gluck: *Alceste Overture;* Handel: *Alcina Over-
ture; Berenice Overture*)

OVERTURE, SCHERZO AND FINALE, OP. 52
(Composed in 1841)

In effect, this is a three-movement symphony.
Though not often performed, it is a really lovely
score. Of all Schumann's orchestral works, this
has the most sweetness and grace, and the first
movement, "overture," has more of a vernal quality than the *Spring* Symphony. Had Schumann
gotten around to a slow movement, he might
have published the score as a symphony. The
scherzo has as much, and probably more, charm
than the equivalent movements of any of the
symphonies, and the finale suggests the powerful
build-up of the *Rhenish.* Of the three LP performances currently available, I prefer the
Kletzki, though each has its points. Kletzki is a
little livelier than Schuricht, though, curiously,
his tempo in the scherzo is slower. Schuricht

seems preferable in that movement. On the whole, Kletzki gets more colorful sounds from his orchestra than any of the others. Schuricht brings a mellow point of view to the score, and a sense of tradition. Collingwood, sober and conscientious, always has matters under expert control. His orchestra, however (or it may be the recording) has a rather thin sound.

——Israel Philharmonic Orchestra, Paul Kletzki, cond. ANGEL 35373 (with *Symphony No. 2*)

——Orchestre du Conservatoire de Paris, Carl Schuricht, cond. LONDON LL 1037 (with *Symphony No. 3*)

——London Symphony Orchestra, Lawrence Collingwood, cond. M-G-M E 3102 (with Brahms: *Academic Festival Overture; Tragic Overture*)

THE FOUR SYMPHONIES (COMPLETE)
(*Symphony No. 1, "Spring," in B-flat, Op. 38, composed in 1841; No. 2, in C, Op. 61, 1845; No. 3, "Rhenish," in E-flat, Op. 97, 1850; No. 4, in D minor, Op. 120, 1841, revised 1851.*)

For the first time in the history of the phonograph, the four Schumann symphonies have been brought together in a single album. The idea is praiseworthy; the results here are disappointing. Generally Boult either speeds off in a great shower of gravel, as in the Third Symphony, or is curiously listless, as in the slow movement of the First. Normally one of the sanest and most dependable of conductors, Boult is singularly unconvincing here, and his interpretations at best cannot be described as much more than routine. Even the heavenly slow movement of the C major, perhaps the most personal effusion Schumann ever penned, is spoiled by Boult's matter-of-fact phrasing and his fast tempo. It remains to be noted that on the album cover Westminster has reproduced September Morn in all her nude prettiness, thus adding a touch of sex for those who think Schumann alone is not enough. Those interested in the music, however, had better turn to individual versions of the symphonies.

——Philharmonic Promenade Orchestra, Sir Adrian Boult, cond. WESTMINSTER XWN 2223, 2 discs. (The symphonies are also available separately: Nos. 1 and 2 on XWN 18670; Nos. 3 and 4 on XWN 18671.)

SYMPHONY NO. 1, IN B-FLAT,
OP. 38 ("SPRING")
(*Composed in 1841*)

Each of the four Schumann symphonies has completely individual characteristics. The *Spring*, No. 1, is the most transparent and happiest of the four, and the opening horn call—did Schumann have *Der Freischütz* in mind?—suggests the vista to a new romantic world. Nothing like this symphony had been written before. It is like an extended song, in classical sonata form only by courtesy. Of the several discs on the market that couple Schumann's First and Fourth Symphonies, the Krips is easily the best. It has a fine quality of recorded sound and a sympathetic musical approach that is without exaggeration. Once in a while the winds play out of tune, and in the first movement of the *Spring* Symphony the triangle brr-rs for all the world like an anxious telephone; but one or two minor mishaps —which can occur in any live performance but which are almost unknown on LP discs—are, for some perverse and contrary reason, actually engaging. At least we know that not every measure is a tape-snip job. The Fricsay disc is also good. More and more, Fricsay continues to impress as one of the most talented of the younger conductors. The *Spring,* as directed by him, is alert-sounding, intelligent, and it conveys the romantic quality of the music. Even the last movement, taken at a faster pace than usual, nevertheless has quality. Too many conductors consider Schumann's orchestral work a good take-off for fantastic temperamental excursions. Not Fricsay, who has temperament but keeps it under control. Incidentally, he takes every repeat, including the one in the last movement (rare). Decca has placed the first two movements on the first side, unfortunately, for the second movement leads directly into the third, and thus continuity is broken. London got the entire symphony on one side; surely Decca could have managed three movements.

The old Ansermet performance is beautifully played, but the *Spring* Symphony occupies the entire disc, and that is pretty short change these days. Kletzki finely conveys the mood of the introduction, but later he becomes eccentric. In the chorale-like section just before the end of the first movement, for instance, he takes a big ritard, and the music suddenly comes to a dead stop. Every conductor takes a ritard there, and rightly, but as Kletzki does it, the results sound embarrassing. And is the languishing tempo to the coda of the scherzo really called for? Leinsdorf's version still sounds clear, despite its 1946 vintage, but it is entirely too businesslike for me. Clarity, yes; color, no. The Remington is a reasonably good low-priced version: a little heavy in the brass and a little heavy on the podium. Nothing very exciting happens, but the music is not misrepresented.

———London Symphony Orchestra, Josef Krips, cond. LONDON LL 1736 (with *Symphony No. 4, in D minor, Op. 120*)

———Berlin Radio Symphony Orchestra, Ferenc Fricsay, cond. DECCA DL 9960 (with Smetana: *Die Moldau*)

———Orchestre de la Suisse Romande, Ernest Ansermet, cond. LONDON LLP 391

——Cleveland Orchestra, Erich Leinsdorf, cond. COLUMBIA ML 4794 (with *Symphony No. 4, in D minor, Op. 120*) NOTE: The *Spring* Symphony was originally issued as a 78-rpm set, later as 10-inch ML 2131.

——Rias Orchestra, Otto Matzerath, cond. REM-INGTON R 180

——Israel Philharmonic Orchestra, Paul Kletzki, cond. ANGEL 35372 (with *Symphony No. 4, in D minor, Op. 120*)

SYMPHONY No. 2, IN C, OP. 61
(*Composed in 1845*)

What marks the Second Symphony is its intensity. The slow movement is considered by many, including this writer, the jewel of Schumann's symphonic composition. It is one of the most personal, elegiac, deeply moving meditations in the entire literature. One spot in the last movement, too, is unusual, even for Schumann. The orchestra builds relentlessly to a climax, and at its very apex, instead of the cumulation of sound one expects, all is released in a mournful clarinet solo over agitated triplet figurations of violins and violas: all passion spent. Szell handles this movement admirably. His is a first-class performance—intelligent and logical, well-proportioned, with brisk but not hurried tempos and, above all, whiplash clarity. It may not be a highly emotional reading, but it must be respected for its honesty and stringent musicianship. The version is dated in sound. Kletzki, who has gorgeous reproduction, uses a heavily retouched scoring. Most conductors add or subtract a part here and there in all of Schumann's orchestral music (he was an inept orchestrator), but Kletzki has selected, or written himself, a wholesale reconstruction. His conducting does not have the mannerisms encountered in his performances of the First and Fourth Symphonies, and his recording of the Second is the only one supplied with a bonus, in the form of the Overture, Scherzo and Finale. Paray uses the original orchestration. He is a methodical conductor without much grace in this symphony, and even the adagio manages to sound prosaic.

——Cleveland Symphony Orchestra, George Szell, cond. COLUMBIA ML 4817

——Israel Philharmonic Orchestra, Paul Kletzki, cond. ANGEL 35373 (with *Overture, Scherzo and Finale*)

——Detroit Symphony Orchestra, Paul Paray, cond. MERCURY MG 50102

SYMPHONY No. 3, IN E-FLAT,
OP. 97 ("RHENISH")
(*Composed in 1850*)

The *Rhenish,* proudest, most muscular and large-scaled of the Schumann symphonies, has a free-swinging quality, with its broad themes and its surging opening, its frank lyricism and the sheer exuberance of its ending. Unfortunately there is no full satisfactory recorded version. The Toscanini, taken from the broadcast of November 12, 1949, is harsh and unresonant in sound. Details are hard to hear and many are completely obscured. (Among the details that *can* be heard is that of Toscanini humming along.) But despite inferior sound, the interpretation is triumphant. Toscanini's is by far the most intense performance ever put on records. Even the third movement, marked by Schumann "nicht schnell," is very schnell indeed. But Toscanini's control, and his ability to maintain a perpetually singing line, prevent the movement from being flip. Kletzki's well-recorded version avoids the romantic excesses to which he subjects some of the other Schumann symphonies in his series. Here he even seems to lean over backwards, and is matter-of-fact where the music cries for a romantic treatment. The third movement is a case in point. Kletzki goes metronomically through instead of caressing the melodies. For the most part, however, a perfectly reliable job. Schuricht's recording is not up to London's best. The sound is edgy, perhaps because of the necessity of getting all five movements on one side. Inner-groove distortion was bound to result. Not unexpectedly, Schuricht's tempos are very fast; with so much to get on one side, something had to give. Little need be said about Zecchi's routine performance, or about Dixon's dull one. The Paray disc suffers from dry, shrill and unresonant sound, almost as bad as the Toscanini disc. But where Toscanini is incandescent, Paray is merely conscientious.

——NBC Symphony, Arturo Toscanini, cond. RCA VICTOR LM 2048

——Israel Philharmonic Orchestra, Paul Kletzki, cond. ANGEL 35374 (with *Manfred Overture*)

——Orchestre du Conservatoire de Paris, Carl Schuricht, cond. LONDON LL 1037 (with *Overture, Scherzo and Finale*)

——Amsterdam Concertgebouw, Carlo Zecchi, cond. EPIC LC 3092.

——Vienna State Opera Orchestra, Dean Dixon, cond. WESTMINSTER XWN 18368 (with *Symphony No. 4, in D minor, Op. 120*)   NOTE: The Third Symphony was originally released as WL 5285.

——Detroit Symphony Orchestra, Paul Paray, cond. MERCURY MG 50133.

SYMPHONY No. 4, IN D MINOR, OP. 120
(*Composed 1841; revised 1851*)

This is probably the most popular of the Schumann symphonies. It is a one-movement work, though in several sections corresponding to the so-called classic pattern, and it anticipates the cyclic form later taken up by Liszt. I find Krips the most satisfactory conductor on LP. He has mellow-sounding recording, and his ideas about the music are sane, sensitive and level-headed. He takes fairly deliberate tempos, letting the melodies expand and sing out, and demanding of his lower strings that they articulate clearly. On the whole he sticks close to the original scoring, though occasionally he "undoubles" a few parts. His is a relaxed view toward the music, and he is able to carry out his easygoing tempos without sounding stodgy. A warm, knowledgeable interpretation, very much worth having. Furtwängler is highly mannered and over-deliberate. He lingers over phrases, he accents where it suits him, and he changes tempos at whim. In the concert hall, with the force of his personality playing over the audience, such idiosyncrasies might well have had an overwhelming impact; but on records it is not apparent, and his version seems twice as long as any other (although, of course, in fact it isn't). Szell's recording is unresonant but clear. As always, he gets beautifully disciplined playing from his orchestra, and the performance is typically intelligent, though cold. Kletzki is at his worst here, conducting languidly, with abrupt changes of tempo; one feels tempted to say "Get on with it, man." Kletzki is a virtuoso conductor, and this tender symphony is not for him. Paray's performance is vigorous and unemotional, and Dixon's has little to contribute.

——London Symphony Orchestra, Josef Krips, cond. LONDON LL 1736 (with *Symphony No. 1, in B-flat, Op. 38*)

——Cleveland Symphony Orchestra, George Szell, cond. COLUMBIA ML 4794 (with *Symphony No. 1, in B-flat, Op. 38*)

——Berlin Philharmonic Orchestra, Wilhelm Furtwängler, cond. DECCA DL 9767 (with Haydn: *Symphony No. 88*)

——Detroit Symphony Orchestra, Paul Paray, cond. MERCURY MG 50036 (with Liszt: *Les Préludes*)

——Vienna State Opera Orchestra, Dean Dixon, cond. WESTMINSTER XWN 18368 (with *Symphony No. 3, in E-flat, Op. 97*) NOTE: The Fourth Symphony was originally released as WL 5285.

Chamber Music

ADAGIO AND ALLEGRO, IN A-FLAT, OP. 70
(*Composed in 1849*)

Several of Schumann's chamber works were
written with alternate instruments in mind. The
present Adagio and Allegro, originally named
Romance and Allegro, was conceived for horn
and piano, but Schumann later signified his
satisfaction with violin or cello alternate. Stagliano plays the original horn version: a novelty,
for concert-goers are familiar with the music
almost entirely through the cello. Yet no matter
how fine the horn player—and Stagliano is one
of the finest—the music somehow manages to
sound unwieldy. His recording is clear but the
disc has a good deal of surface noise. Janigro,
playing the cello version, has a romantic conception, and one wishes that his tone had the
warm hue needed to put his ideas into effect.
It is full enough but decidedly on the dry side.
Such accurate and sensitive playing as Janigro
offers, however, puts his disc on any recommended list. Excellent recorded sound. Ansermet

183

has orchestrated the Adagio and Allegro, with Edmond Leloir as the horn soloist, on LONDON LL 3020 (with a Mozart flute concerto and Haydn's Trumpet Concerto in C). The transcription is tasteful, but the originals are recommended.

——Antonio Janigro, cello; Eugenio Bagnoli, piano. WESTMINSTER XWN 18016 (with *Fünf Stücke im Volkston; Fantasiestücke, Op. 73;* Schubert: *Arpeggione Sonata*)

——James Stagliano, horn; Paul Ulanowsky, piano. BOSTON 200 (with Beethoven, Mozart, Schubert)

FANTASIESTÜCKE, OP. 73
(*Composed in 1849*)

This is another work intended for several alternate instruments. It was originally for clarinet and piano, but has been taken over by cellists. Perhaps Schumann had a cello alternate in mind from the very beginning; some authorities say yes, others no. The set consists of three *Fantasiestücke* (fantasy pieces), each short and very much in the mood and style of the piano pieces of the same name. Kell, of course, plays the clarinet version. For my taste he is too wishy-washy. Seemingly he is eternally concentrating on tonal beauty, smooth phrasing, and on an oily legato: all very well in themselves, but not at the expense of passion and inner life. And these ultra-romantic pieces demand an impassioned approach. Janigro plays with his usual competence, and his version is preferred. Parisot achieves some lyric moments, but his playing lacks strength and often is over-sweet. A splendid version by Maurice Gendron, on LONDON LL 654, has been withdrawn.

——Antonio Janigro, cello; Eugenio Bagnoli, piano. WESTMINSTER XWN 18016 (with *Adagio and Allegro, in A-flat, Op. 70; Fünf Stücke im Volkston;* Schubert: *Arpeggione Sonata*)

——Aldo Parisot, cello; Leopold Mittman, piano. OVERTONE 16 (with Debussy: *Sonata for Cello and Piano, in D minor;* Mendelssohn: *Sonata for Cello and Piano No. 2, in D, Op. 58*)

——Reginald Kell, clarinet; Joel Rosen, piano. DECCA DL 9744 (with Weber: **Grand Duo;** Debussy: *Rhapsody No. 1*)

FÜNF STÜCKE IM VOLKSTON, OP. 102
(*Composed in 1849*)

The title means "Five Pieces in Folk-Song Style." I do not know if they are original folk melodies, though they do have a folk character (albeit one put through Schumann's romantic blender). They are short, simple and tuneful. Both of the LP performances of the complete set are good. Janigro plays with spirit and grace, handicapped by a tone that is not as rich as it might be. Casals brings a more personal kind of playing, and some might even call it a more mannered style. But whatever one thinks of the Casals mannerisms, and of the awesome grunts and groans that accompany his playing, his authority cannot be denied. The size and mellowness of tone he draws from his instrument are something that hardly a living cellist could duplicate. Rostropovich plays only three of the five pieces—Nos. 1, 3 and 4. Perhaps these are the only ones he has studied; on a now discontinued London-International disc (TW 91068) he also played the same three. Both performances are much the same. They feature a good deal of rubato (though less than Casals uses), plenty of leeway in tempo, a stylish sense of phrase and musical refinement. It is a pity that he has not recorded the entire set.

——Pablo Casals, cello; Leopold Mannes, piano. COLUMBIA ML 4718 (with *Trio No. 1, in D minor, Op. 63*)   NOTE: The *Fünf Stücke* are also available in the 3-disc SL 184, which contains music of Schumann and Brahms made at the Prades Festival.

——Antonio Janigro, cello; Eugenio Bagnoli, piano. WESTMINSTER XWN 18016 (with *Adagio and Allegro, in A-flat, Op. 70;* Schubert: *Arpeggione Sonata*)

——Mstislav Rostropovich, cello; Vladimir Yampolsky, piano. WESTMINSTER XWN 18688 (with encore pieces)

INTERMEZZO
(*Composed in 1853*)

This sounds like the title of a film. It is a movement from a violin sonata that Schumann, Brahms and Dietrich (a pupil of Schumann's) composed jointly for Joachim. Milstein, on his disc, plays only the Intermezzo, Schumann's portion. Stern plays the entire sonata. Both performances are excellent. The Stern, however, can be obtained only in the two-disc set of the Brahms violin sonatas.

——Nathan Milstein, violin; Carlo Bussotti, piano. CAPITOL P 8259 (with encore pieces)
——Isaac Stern, violin; Alexander Zakin, piano. In COLUMBIA SL 202, 2 discs (with Brahms: *Three Violin Sonatas*)

MÄRCHENERZÄHLUNGEN, OP. 132
(*Composed in 1853*)

A long German word that means "fairy tales." Schumann's *Märchenerzählungen* are a set of four pieces scored for piano, clarinet, and viola—a fairly unusual combination. So is the music itself fairly unusual. It is never heard in concert. Even in these LP days, when the most out-of-the-way items have been recorded several times, this disc, which was recorded in 1950 (one of Westminster's very first discs), remains the sole available version. Yet the music is utterly charming: Schumann at his most relaxed and genial, with the inevitable harmonic invention, and the deceptive simplicity of melodic structure. The performance is very much worth investigating, especially in the expert presentation of the Viennese players. On the reverse of the disc are Mendelssohn's *Konzertstücke*, also an out-of-the-way item worth making acquaintance.

——Joerg Demus, piano; Leopold Wlach, clarinet; Erich Weiss, viola. WESTMINSTER XWN 18494 (with Mendelssohn: *Konzertstücke*) NOTE: This disc was originally released as WL 5024.

QUARTET FOR STRINGS No. 1, IN A MINOR, OP. 41, No. 1
(*Composed in 1842*)

Aside from the Piano Quintet, Schumann's chamber music has never been popular, as witness the paucity of available recordings. Yet the three string quartets have noble ideas, and they breathe Schumann's ever-present romanticism. They also have a fascinating contrapuntal interplay. The story of Schumann as a contrapuntalist has not been fully written. He had made a life-long study of Bach, and at one time he wrote to Clara that he himself thought polyphonically and that in all of his music there were contrapuntal threads linking the thematic material. The A minor Quartet starts off with a strict canon before wandering off into the specific substance of sonata form. Another point: the three quartets thematically are very similar to the symphonies, and if you like one, you should like the other. (Again there is room for a thorough study of thematic resemblances between quartet and symphony in Schumann.) But don't expect the Mozart-Schubert-Beethoven approach to the string quartet. Schumann's philosophy was entirely different. The slow (third) movement of the A minor Quartet is nothing but a long song. Even Schubert attempted more in his slow movements. I am not happy with the only exemplar of the A minor Quartet in the catalogues. The Curtis Quartet is apt to be a little heavy and over-deliberate, and its intonation is not precisely adjusted. They suggest the basic quality of the music, however, and the recorded sound is exceptionally realistic.

——Curtis String Quartet. WESTMINSTER XWN 18495 (with *Quartet for Strings No. 3, in A, Op. 41, No. 3*) NOTE: This disc was originally issued as WL 5166.

QUARTET FOR STRINGS No. 2,
IN F, OP. 41, No. 2
(*Composed in 1842*)

Both versions discussed here have been discontinued, and are mentioned only for the sake of completeness. Notable in this quartet is a pervading lyricism. The wide-arched span of the melody that opens the work, soaring well over an octave, immediately sets the mood, and it is a mood seldom broken during the course of the music. Anybody interested in the work should make an effort to locate the Quartetto Italiano disc (here the players are named the New Italian Quartet). The New Music Quartet is downright aggressive in its approach. It has received better recorded sound, however; the London disc has a strong background hum. A good recording of the F major Quartet (and of the other two, also) is badly needed.

——New Italian String Quartet. LONDON LLP 323 (with Verdi: *Quartet for Strings, in E minor*)

——New Music String Quartet. COLUMBIA ML 4982 (with *Quartet No. 3, in A, Op. 41, No. 3*)

QUARTET FOR STRINGS No. 3,
IN A, OP. 41, No. 3
(*Composed in 1842*)

This is my favorite of the three quartets. The first movement, dominated by the plaintive, descending F-sharp-B motto, has a strong and well-developed polyphonic texture. The second movement is a long sigh, and Freudians undoubtedly will be able to make something of the gasping characteristic of the rhythm. There is a remarkable chromatic texture to the adagio, and

—breaking the mood—an overwhelming *joie de vivre* in the finale, with themes hurtling pell-mell atop one another. There is only one version of the score, now that the New Music Quartet's performance on Columbia ML 4982 has been discontinued. The Curtis Quartet favors slow tempos and tends to linger over phrases. More life is needed, more of the romantic impulse. And also a tighter ensemble.

——Curtis String Quartet. WESTMINSTER XWN 18495 (with *Quartet for Strings No. 1, in A minor, Op. 41, No. 1*) NOTE: This disc was originally issued as WL 5166.

QUARTET FOR PIANO AND STRINGS,
IN E-FLAT, OP. 47
(*Composed in 1842*)

The New York Quartet consists of Mieczyslaw Horszowski, piano; Alexander Schneider, violin; Milton Katims, viola, and Frank Miller, cello. They play well together, as should be expected of four such experienced musicians. Only in the slow movement is there a noticeable drag, and one wonders if the fault is not as much the composer's as the musicians'. For this is not one of Schumann's more inspired pieces of music. He sounds here as though he is working by formula. The Westminster disc does not present the music in too favorable a light. Demus, the pianist of the ensemble, is quite literal, and every note

comes through with accuracy. But he is more muscular than poetic, lacking in color and style. The Barylli Quartet members have raw tonal characteristics: the strings sound edgy, and seldom is there a graceful turn of phrase, especially in the second movement. It should sound light and delicate; here it comes out stiff. As for Bohle and the Barchet Quartet players, they approach the music with a paralyzing ponderousness. They are so *echt Deutsch* as to be virtually parodistic.
——New York Quartet. COLUMBIA ML 4892 (with Brahms: *Trio for Horn, Piano and Cello, in E-flat, Op. 40*)
——Joerg Demus, piano; Members of the Barylli Quartet. WESTMINSTER XWN 18575 (with *Quintet for Piano and Strings, in E-flat, Op. 44*)
——Walter Bohle, piano. Members of the Barchet Quartet. Vox PL 8960 (with *Quintet for Piano and Strings, in E-flat, Op. 44*)

QUINTET FOR PIANO AND STRINGS,
IN E-FLAT, OP. 44
(*Composed in 1842*)

If you like the piano concerto and somehow have missed the Piano Quintet, you should rush right out and buy yourself a copy. The E-flat Quintet is a baby sister of the concerto, stylistically sibling in many details (except, of course, in sonority and actual melodic ideas; but the melodies of the quintet are every bit as strongly

pronounced as those of the concerto). As in
much of the chamber music, there is a good deal
of polyphonic writing, and in the last movement
Schumann goes so far as to juggle several themes
together, including the proud statement that
opens the work. Ever since Gabrilowitsch and
the Flonzaley Quartet recorded the work in pre-
electric days it has attracted superior exponents.
My favorite LP performance of this masterpiece
has been dropped—Rubinstein and the Paganini
Quartet (RCA Victor LM 1095, originally recorded on shellac discs). If you come across it,
don't ask questions but grab; more than any
version it captures the glow and surge of the
score. It is an excellent-sounding specimen of
recorded sound, too, and never should have been
discontinued. Curzon, with the Budapest Quartet,
is dependable, musicianly, and just a little stodgy.
It is as though he were so determined to enter
into the room of chamber ensemble that he
checked his own personality at the door. The
work, too, occupies an entire disc, whereas subsequent recordings offer two works for the
price of Columbia's one. But Columbia has
supplemented its Curzon-Budapest by one made
in Prades by an illustrious group of players
headed by Myra Hess; and they manage to get
the work on one side with Brahms' lovely G
major String Quintet on the other. It is a good,
though not outstanding performance; you can't

take a group of players, no matter how distinguished, and weld them into a great chamber-music ensemble during one summer. The Capitol disc I find tricky: too many cute ritards, underlinings, lily-gildings and over-interpretation in general. It ends up sounding very affected. The best that can be said of the Westminster disc is that it is competent. The string playing, however, is labored in spots (*cf.* the section after the first repeat in the second movement). Nor is the intonation of the group uniformly accurate. As for Bohle-Barchet, they have a kind of Teutonic thoroughness, something like a tank going through a field of lilies.

——Myra Hess, piano; Isaac Stern, Alexander Schneider, violinists; Milton Thomas, viola; Paul Tortelier, cello. Columbia ML 4711 (with Brahms: *Quintet for Strings, in G, Op. 111*) Note: Both works are also contained in SL 182, a three-disc set of Schumann and Brahms made at the Prades Festival.

——Clifford Curzon, piano; Budapest String Quartet. Columbia ML 4426.

——Joerg Demus, piano; Barylli String Quartet. Westminster XWN 18575 (with *Quartet for Piano and Strings, in E-flat, Op. 47*)

——Walter Bohle, piano; Barchet String Quartet. Vox PL 8960 (with *Quartet for Piano and Strings, in E-flat, Op. 47*)

——Victor Aller, piano; Hollywood String

Quartet. CAPITOL P 8316 (with Hummel: *Quartet for Strings, in G*)

SONATA FOR VIOLIN AND PIANO No. 1,
IN A MINOR, OP. 105
(*Composed in 1851*)

The usual Schumann spontaneity and romanticism come through some rather rambling writing. But despite many felicities, the two Schumann violin sonatas have never been favorites. Of the two, the A minor is the superior effort. Its opening theme is gorgeous and, as in so many of the late works, there is a plaintive, pleading, yearning quality. The players on the Westminster disc are unknown to Americans; they have never appeared in this country and this is their first LP disc. They are a pair of artists with considerable sympathy for the romantic style. Doukan is a smooth instrumentalist who thinks in long phrases and bows with considerable elegance. He has a superior technique, a fine, warm tone, and impeccable intonation. His partner is much more subtle than the general run of sonata "accompanists." She makes as much music as he does; and though she integrates perfectly with his playing, she retains her own individuality. Another reason for putting the Westminster disc at the top is that it contains the only LP version of the Schumann D minor Violin Sonata, and what more appropriate coupling could there be? Goldberg's disc also contains the Brahms D minor Sonata, of which there are several superior interpretations. Goldberg, as always, plays with sensitive musicianship. The only reservation I have concerns his treatment of the first movement, which is scarcely the *allegro appassionata* indicated by the composer. But even here there is a good amount of cultured playing. Druian's playing is more sluggish than Doukan's or Goldberg's, and his intonation is not always in perfect order. The Ajemian sisters, thoroughly competent as they are, fail to match Doukan and Goldberg in precision of style.

——Pierre Doukan, violin; Françoise Petit, piano. WESTMINSTER XWN 18631 (with *Sonata for Violin and Piano No. 2, in D minor, Op. 121*)

——Szymon Goldberg, violin; Artur Balsam, piano. DECCA DL 9721 (with Brahms: *Sonata for Violin and Piano No. 3, in D minor, Op. 108*)

——Anahid Ajemian, violin; Maro Ajemian, piano. M-G-M E 3383 (with Schubert: *Fantasy for Violin and Piano, in C, Op. 159*)

——Rafael Druian, violin; John Simms, piano. MERCURY MG 50091 (with Brahms: *Sonata for Violin and Piano No. 2, in G, Op. 78*)

SONATA FOR VIOLIN AND PIANO No. 2,
IN D MINOR, OP. 121
(*Composed in 1851*)

In this dark-sounding but ineffectual D minor

Sonata, the composer never gets off the ground. It deserves a recording however, just as, say, an ineffectual play like *Pericles* deserved publication. There are those who are interested in everything a certain composer, or dramatist, has written. Doukan and Petit give a warm, sympathetic performance. See remarks directly above as to their general style.

——Pierre Doukan, violin; Françoise Petit, piano; WESTMINSTER XWN 18631 (with *Sonata for Violin and Piano No. 1, in A minor, Op. 105*)

TRIO FOR PIANO AND STRINGS No. 1,
IN D MINOR, OP. 63
(*Composed in 1847*)

This is easily the most popular of the three Schumann piano trios. Nos. 2 and 3 are seldom heard. Perhaps some of its popularity stems from the famous old (*c.* 1927) Cortot-Casals-Thibaud performance, which Victor made available on LP some years ago on LCT 1141 but which is no longer in circulation. The music is among Schumann's most dramatic, dark-hued creations. Of the three available discs, the Columbia and Decca run neck and neck. The former is a warmer interpretation, highly romantic, with considerable leeway in matters of tempo and phrasing. The latter is an old but still clear-sounding recording. The musicians on the Decca disc produce a thinner sound than Casals and his cohorts. They are, however, sharper in musical outline; emotionally perhaps a trifle reserved, but always lyric and musicianly. Rough tone and ensemble prevail in the Vox disc.

——Alexander Schneider, violin; Pablo Casals, cello; Mieczyslaw Horszowski, piano; COLUMBIA ML 4718 (with *Fünf Stücke im Volkston, Op. 102*) NOTE: The D minor Trio is also available in the three-disc SL 184, which contains music of Schumann and Brahms made at the Prades Festival.

——Bronislaw Gimpel, violin; Luigi Silva, cello; Leopold Mannes, piano. DECCA DL 9604 (with Schubert: *Nocturne, in E-flat, Op. 148*)

——Trio di Bolzano. Vox PL 9920 (with *Trio for Piano and Strings No. 3, in G minor, Op. 110*)

TRIO FOR PIANO AND STRINGS No. 2,
IN F, OP. 80
(*Composed in 1847*)

I am mentioning this discontinued disc for the sake of completeness, since it provided the only LP recording ever made of the F major Trio. It was, unfortunately, not a good performance, but those who desire discographic completeness should know of its existence if they want to search it out.

——Trio di Bolzano. Vox PL 8480 (with Chopin: *Trio for Piano and Strings, in G minor, Op. 8*)

TRIO FOR PIANO AND STRINGS No. 3,
IN G MINOR, OP. 110
(*Composed in 1851*)

A weak work, and a weak performance of it. Granted that the music is diffuse, but a stronger and more assertive ensemble than the Trio di Bolzano might have been able to bring the music together with more conviction.

——Trio di Bolzano. Vox PL 9920 (with *Trio for Piano and Strings No. 1, in D minor, Op. 63*)

Piano Works

ABEGG VARIATIONS, OP. 1
(*Composed in 1830*)

What an Op. 1 this is! All the main facets of Schumann's style are present, including a title based on the name of a young lady (Fraülein Meta Abegg, a dancing partner at a Mannheim ball). The composition, of course, is not mature and contains some naïvetés. Yet toward the end of the piece occur some ravishing examples of piano writing unlike anything being done in Europe at the time (Chopin in Poland always excepted). And the piece strongly announced Schumann's particular kind of romanticism and the form it was to take. It is nowhere near as weak as some analysts would have one think. The only recorded version fails to bring out the special character of the piece. Demus plays the notes accurately, but he simply does not have the tone or imagination to vitalize it. Serkin once gave a wonderful performance at a Carnegie Hall recital. Perhaps he will eventually get around to recording it.

——Joerg Demus. WESTMINSTER XWN 18061
(with *Arabesque, Op. 18; Blumenstück, Op. 14;
Faschingsschwank aus Wien, Op. 26*)

ANDANTE AND VARIATIONS IN B-FLAT,
FOR TWO PIANOS, OP. 46
(*Composed in 1843*)

Schumann originally composed this wistful and
appealing work for the unlikely combination of
two pianos, two cellos and horn. (It was so
recorded by Appleton and Field, and supporting
instrumentalists, on Vox PL 7740, now discontinued.) Nobody presents it in that form any
more, and it has developed into a staple of the
two-piano repertory. Schumann himself must
have known that the original version did not
"work," and when he recast it for two pianos he
even dropped one of the variations. More brilliant two-piano works have been composed—
Chopin's Rondo in C is one—but few that have
the inner glow of the Andante and Variations.
The only really decent interpretation on LP
comes from Luboshutz and Nemenoff, who at
least have some idea of the music's romanticism.
But their recording was made many years ago,
and its restoration on the Camden disc is muffled
in sound and badly distorted. Bartlett and
Robertson pick at the notes rather than play
them. They seem reluctant to use any color or
pedal effects, and they end up sounding singu-

larly thin. Ferrante and Teicher are brittle, seemingly interested only in a mechanical exposition
of the notes. A modern recording of this lovely
work is badly needed. Wouldn't it be nice if two
great pianists—Horowitz and Rubinstein, say—
joined forces in two-piano work the way
Gabrilowitsch and Bauer did, and Rosenthal and
Joseffy before *them?*

——Pierre Luboshutz and Genia Nemenoff.
RCA CAMDEN 206 (with Brahms: *Variations on
a Theme by Haydn, Op. 56b;* Saint-Saëns: *Variations on a Theme by Beethoven;* Mendelssohn-
Luboshutz: *Allegro Brillant*) NOTE: These
were originally recorded on 78-rpm discs.

——Ethel Bartlett and Rae Robertson. M-G-M E
3027 (with Brahms: *Variations on a Theme by
Haydn, Op. 56b; Waltzes, Op. 39*)

——Louis Teicher and Arthur Ferrante. WEST-
MINSTER XWN 18169 (with Brahms: *Variations
on a Theme by Haydn, Op. 56b;* Saint-Saëns:
Variations on a Theme by Beethoven)

ARABESQUE, OP. 18
(*Composed in 1838*)

Apparently Schumann was the first composer to
use the word "arabesque" as a title. One might
expect all kinds of filigree with that title in mind,
but nothing of the sort occurs. The *Arabesque*
opens with a theme of a simple melodious nature,
and there are several contrasting episodes. In
1956 there were in the catalogue six available

versions; now there is only one, and that one is not particularly exhilarating. Demus is efficient and methodical, but he does not begin to suggest the plastic quality of the piece. Of the discontinued versions, the Kempff (LONDON LL 515) is worth making an effort to locate. He brings fluidity and elegance to the *Arabesque:* an ability to lift a phrase and then let it subside. The greatest performance ever recorded of this work belongs to Horowitz. It never was transferred to LP, but if anyone can locate 10-inch VICTOR 1713 he will get a magical, poised and wonderfully poetic performance. It is one of Horowitz' very special recordings.

——Joerg Demus. WESTMINSTER XWN 18061 (with *Abegg Variations, Op. 1; Blumenstück, Op. 14; Faschingsschwank aus Wien, Op. 26*)

BLUMENSTÜCK, OP. 14
(*Composed in 1839*)

Seldom does this piece turn up in concert. In fact, in many years of attendance at the concert hall, I have never encountered it. The title means "Flower Piece." It is a lyric work, somewhat repetitious, and fairly unimportant in the Schumann canon. Both of its recorded performances are fair. Pressler is a little more lyrical and gives more attention to shadings, while Demus is more powerful and more precise in his dynamics. Both versions, too, have fine recorded sound. I would suggest the Demus version because it contains the only available LP performance of the delicious *Abegg* Variations.

——Joerg Demus. WESTMINSTER XWN 18061 (with *Abegg Variations, Op. 1; Faschingsschwank aus Wien, Op. 26; Arabesque, Op. 18*)

——Menahem Pressler. M-G-M E 3029 (with *Romances, Op. 28;* Mendelssohn: *Variations sérieuses; Rondo capriccioso*)

BUNTE BLÄTTER, OP. 99
(*Composed between 1832 and 1849*)

Another Schumann rarity, and quite a lovely one. Why pianists have ignored this attractive series of sketches is hard to say. The set consists of fourteen pieces, of which Haskil plays the first eight, as a filler for the Schubert sonata that occupies most of the disc. She plays well, with obvious sympathy for the delicate nature of the music. A complete version is long overdue. The title, by the way, means "Leaves of a Variegated Color." Schumann put together a group of piano pieces that he had composed over a long interval and did not exactly know what to do with.

——Clara Haskil. EPIC LC 3031 (with Schubert: *Sonata in B-flat, posth.*)

CARNAVAL, OP. 9
(*Composed in 1834-35*)

Schumann's most popular piano piece and one of the cornerstones of the romantic piano repertoire, the *Carnaval* is whimsical, fantastic, robust music. Ideas tumble over ideas; there is not an uninteresting phrase anywhere in the work. It demands a pianist steeped in the romantic tradition, and it also needs a first-rate technician (the *Paganini* section, with its wide leaps, is one of the most hazardous exercises a pianist has to face in the literature). A line has to be drawn between sentiment (of which there is much) and sentimentality (of which there is none); and the pianist must also be an accomplished colorist. Schumann composed a few of the sections of the *Carnaval* with tongue in cheek, and the pianist must also be responsive to those. The entire work is based on four notes—A, S (E-flat), C, and H (B-natural), in various permutations. Asch is the name of a town in Germany where lived a young lady who interested the composer. He introduced into the writing not only the town but friends of his—Chopin, Paganini, the young lady in question (*Estrella*), himself (*Florestan* and *Eusebius*), Clara Wieck (*Chiarina*), and others. He ends with a rousing *March of the Davidsbund Against the Philistines*. To Schumann, the reactionary element in musical life was, to the very end, the Philistine; and he (assisted by his friends) was the young David who was going to be the slayer. It's all very fanciful and very, very romantic. And *Carnaval* is also very great music.

The catalogues in recent years have suffered a tremendous mortality in *Carnavals*. Within two years, versions by Anda (on London-Telefunken; Anda's Angel disc remains), Arrau, Sandor, Cortot, Magaloff, and Pressler have been deleted. None of these, however, was of great importance. The exemplar, fortunately, remains. I refer to the Rachmaninoff disc. Of all the versions ever recorded, it seems to me that the Rachmaninoff (made on April 12, 1929) has always left competition far behind. His conception is gigantic. His tempos are inclined to be faster than those customary today, and he is a little chary of pedal effects (or is that the fault of the aged recording?). But the virility of his playing, his sheer grasp of the notes, his power in climaxes, his personal way of molding a phrase, the general authority and finish of the pianism—these are qualities that no living player seems able to duplicate. The charge of mannerism may be leveled against it by the younger generation, and it is true that the playing has its arbitrary moments. It is also true that Rachmaninoff makes the mistake of playing the *Sphinxes*, which Schumann inserted into the music as his little joke. (They supply the clue to the A,S,C,H, mottos, and are not intended to be played.) But nothing like this *Carnaval* has ever been put on records. Of more recent interpretations, I incline to the Novaes, a delicate interpretation, feminine

in the best sense of the word, with considerable
subtlety and nuance. On this disc the sound is a
little dated, but it still can serve. The disc was
originally issued in March, 1951, as Vox PL
6710 (with Chopin's Sonata in B-flat minor) but
was transferred to its present number a year or
so later. Rubinstein's version, to which one had
looked forward with such anticipation, is a little
disappointing. The grand manner is present, but
also a curious stodginess and deliberation. There
are some wonderful moments, but the total effect
remains negative and even unconvincing. Even
more unconvincing is Anda, who indulges in
some surprising immaturities. How a pianist
could play the *Carnaval* so badly and the *Études
symphoniques* so well is another of life's little
mysteries.

Gieseking, who seldom plays badly, offers a
steady *Carnaval* that is just a shade noncommittal
and not altogether accurate technically. It is
obviously the playing of an experienced pianist,
but the element of rapture is missing. I would
avoid the stiff Brailowsky performance, and also
the Badura-Skoda disc, which offers routine playing lacking in personality. Casadesus is fast, even
breathless, and he rattles along in an efficient but
superficial manner.

——Sergei Rachmaninoff. RCA CAMDEN CAL
396 (with Chopin: *Sonata in B-flat minor, Op.
35*) NOTE: Originally recorded on 78-rpm

discs and then transferred to 10-in. LCT 12.

——Guiomar Novaes. Vox PL 7830 (with *Papillons, Op. 2*) NOTE: Originally released on PL 6710.

——Artur Rubinstein. RCA VICTOR LM 1822 (with Franck: *Prelude, Chorale and Fugue*)

——Walter Gieseking. COLUMBIA ML 4772 (with Mozart: *Piano Sonatas Nos. 14 in C minor, K. 457, and 15 in C, K. 545*)

——Paul Badura-Skoda. WESTMINSTER XWN 18490 (with *Sonata No. 1, in F-sharp minor, Op. 11*) NOTE: Originally issued as WL 5105.

——Geza Anda. ANGEL 35247 (with *Kreisleriana, Op. 16*)

——Robert Casadesus. COLUMBIA ML 5146 (with *Fantasia, in C, Op. 17*)

——Alexander Brailowsky. RCA VICTOR LM 9003 (with *Fantasia in C, Op. 17*)

CONCERT STUDIES ON CAPRICES BY PAGANINI, OP. 10
(*Composed in 1833*)

When Paganini burst on the scene, he inspired all soloists to do for their instrument what he did for the violin. Like all the romantics, Schumann took Paganini very seriously, and his collected writings are heavily dotted with remarks about the fabulous Italian virtuoso and composer (Paganini was a much better composer than he is generally given credit for being). And thus

Schumann decided to transcribe for the piano some of the Paganini caprices for solo violin. He even did what for him was unprecedented—he reviewed his own six transcriptions in the *Neue Zeitschrift für Musik*. Schumann confessed that his transcriptions were very difficult and concluded, not so modestly, that "they contain so much geniality that it is impossible that those who should have once heard them executed perfectly should not often think of them with pleasure." Schumann undoubtedly reviewed them himself because he thought they were such a departure in bravura technique—as indeed they were—that nobody else would be able to gauge them. Not long afterwards, Liszt's studies on the Paganini caprices were published, and Schumann impartially reviewed *them* too. He was excited about them, but did suggest one point: "Though Schumann's arrangement was intended to bring out the poetic side of [the music], that of Liszt, without ignoring its poetry, rather aims at placing virtuosity in relief." Which is true, except that Schumann's transcriptions are almost as devilishly difficult as Liszt's.

Wuehrer is the first pianist in history to bring all six of Schumann's Studies after Paganini to records. He is a formidable virtuoso but a rather heavy one. He gets through the notes, yet he sounds thick. One longs for a more volatile approach. Nevertheless, he is an honest pianist

who never resorts to meretricious effects, and in
his hands a large measure of the essential quality
of the music emerges. His disc is especially interesting in that he juxtaposes Schumann's dis-
sertations on Paganini with Paganini studies by
Liszt and Brahms, thus presenting the ideas of
three composers on one subject. The recorded
sound on this disc is rather soggy, especially in
the bass.
——Friedrich Wuehrer. Vox PL 8850 (with
Liszt: *Paganini Étude, in A minor*; Brahms:
Paganini Variations, Op. 35).

DAVIDSBÜNDLERTÄNZE, OP. 6
(Composed in 1837)

The Davidites was the name of a club Schumann
invented, peopling it with his friends and asso-
ciates and making its aim the slaying of the
Goliath of Philistinism. The *Davidsbündlertänze*
is a piece of music dealing with this club, and
Schumann has initialed several of the pieces with
an E or an F. *Eusebius* is the name Schumann
gave himself to represent the dreamy, poetic side
of his nature, while Florestan represents the
energetic, ebullient side. (Florestan and Eusebius
also turn up in the *Carnaval*.) It's all a harmless
game at which we can smile paternally. Later, in
the second edition of the work, Schumann
thought the better of the game—possibly he was
a little embarrassed—and removed the initials,

plus all comments in prose and poetry that dotted the first edition. In any case, the *Davidsbündler-tänze* is a wonderful collection of "dances" in which wit, tenderness and joy run freely. I would place it next to the *Carnaval* and the Fantasia in C as the peak of Schumann's piano writing. Several good versions have been dropped from the catalogues, including the really fine one by Adrian Aeschbacher on 10-inch Decca DL 7531. (A discontinued Gieseking disc, on Urania 7106, was issued under questionable circumstances, and the pianist himself disowned it.) Of the available versions, the best is Firkusny's, though it is not the answer to a thoroughly satisfactory edition. He has a good deal of style, yet seems to gloss over some sections in a superficial manner. He takes a 16-measure cut in No. 9, and another cut in No. 15, the latter sanctioned by the first edition of the music. Wuehrer is entirely too solemn for the fluctuating moods of the music. He is an able pianist but not a very effervescent one; and an artist without whimsy, as Wuehrer seems to be, is lost in music like the *Davidsbündlertänze*. Battista tries to overpower the work, banging out the measures in Lisztian fashion; and Demus is merely dull. (A curious recording, now out of print, is Apollo 1, in which the late Adelaide de Lara is the pianist. She was a pupil of Clara Schumann, and perhaps she was an authority on the music, but you would not guess it from her feeble playing.)

——Rudolf Firkusny. CAPITOL P 8337 (with *Études symphoniques, Op. 13*)

——Friedrich Wuehrer. Vox PL 8860 (with *Sonata for Piano No. 3, in F minor, Op. 14*)

——Joseph Battista. M-G-M E 3011

——Joerg Demus. WESTMINSTER XWN 18491 (with *Papillons, Op. 2*)   NOTE: Originally issued as WL 5232.

ÉTUDES SYMPHONIQUES, OP. 13
(*Composed in 1834*)

One of Schumann's most-played works, the *Études symphoniques* is also known as *Symphonic Variations*. What happened was that the composer, in a later edition, changed the title of *Études symphoniques* to *Études en forme de variations*. The work is, in effect, a set of variations on a theme supplied by an amateur. Most of the variations are short (though Schumann has indicated many repeats). He also originally composed five extra variations, some of them extremely beautiful, but he did not include these in any edition, figuring that the work was long enough as it stood. Only within recent years have the posthumous variations made their way into the concert hall, and they are not played by any of the older generation of pianists, who studied the *Études symphoniques* two generations or so ago and are not going to start learning new ones.

Three veteran pianists have, in fact, made beautiful recordings *sans* these posthumous variations. Novaes is the most pianistic of the three; the notes roll from her fingers in a melting sequence. She is frequently unorthodox in her phrasing and general conception, but she is one of the few who can make her own rules. And after one's ears become oriented, it is hard to disagree with her premise. She obviously feels that the variations are improvisatory, and so she plays them, with beautiful control and the singing Novaes tone. Kempff takes every single repeat except the first one in the finale. His playing has poetry and suavity, plus a certain dignity that is not inappropriate to the music. A fine job. Hess, in her disc, illustrates the experience of some forty years before the public. She never need bang the piano to make a point. Her touch is mellow, and so are her musical ideas. She plays the *Études symphoniques* in a leisurely fashion, taking most repeats (she is about five minutes longer than Novaes), dwelling fondly over details, and, as in Étude 10, substituting finesse for strength. She never makes an ugly sound, and her legato does honor to Schumann's melodic line.

That Geza Anda has a big potential is proved by his performance of the work. Whereas in the *Carnaval* and *Kreisleriana* he was sentimental and exaggerated, his playing here has point, and he avoids the mannered, artificial phrasing formerly in evidence. The only major objection one could make concerns his affectations in the slow second variation. He plays two of the five posthumous variations. Anda has more pianistic flair than Badura-Skoda, who plays carefully, accurately, and unexcitingly. It is a tasteful account of the music, however, and anybody who decides on Badura-Skoda should have no real cause for regret. He plays four of the posthumous variations. Boukoff is the only pianist who plays all five. His performance is stern, powerful, and devoid of charm. It is accomplished playing, but somehow not very interesting. Firkusny's disc is disappointing. In Variation II he is strangely mannered, tickling the music and refusing to allow it to flow naturally; and his right-hand articulation in Variation III is not clear. Some of the variations come through beautifully, but the general impression here is that the playing lacks depth. Brailowsky adopts his usual percussive approach, which does not help the music, and Katchen skims smoothly over the surface without once digging in. Graffman is miscast here. He is an intelligent, brilliantly equipped and very serious pianist, but he fails to realize the fluctuations of the variations, and neither tonally nor emotionally does his performance come up to the required standards.

——Guiomar Novaes. Vox PL 10170 (with *Fantasiestücke*, Op. 12)

——Wilhelm Kempff. Decca DL 9948 (with *Kreisleriana, Op. 16*)

——Myra Hess. Angel 35591 (with encore pieces)

——Geza Anda. Angel 35046 (with Brahms: *Variations on a Theme by Paganini, Op. 35*)

——Paul Badura-Skoda. Westminster XWN 18138 (with *Kinderscenen, Op. 15*)

——Yuri Boukoff. Epic LC 3094 (with *Fantasia in C, Op. 17*)

——Rudolf Firkusny. Capitol P 8337 (with *Davidsbündlertänze, Op. 6*)

——Alexander Brailowsky. RCA Victor LM 6000, 2 discs (with Chopin: *Études, Op. 10 and Op. 25*)

——Julius Katchen. London LL 823 (with Franck: *Prelude, Chorale and Fugue*)

——Gary Graffman. RCA Victor LM 2190 (with *Sonata for Piano No. 2, in G minor, Op. 22*)

FANTASIA IN C, OP. 17
(*Composed in 1836*)

Most scholars, critics and music lovers would call this the greatest of all the Schumann piano pieces. Schumann himself realized that it was "the most passionate thing I have ever composed," as he said in a letter to Clara. He intended calling the work a sonata, but its unconventionality (it ends with a slow movement) may have frightened the publishers. Anyway, it was published as a fantasia. Originally Schumann gave a clue to the three movements: *Ruins*, *Triumphal March*, and *Starry Crown*. These too were deleted, and instead a quotation from Schlegel was prefixed to the work. "Through all the tones that sound in earth's fitful dream, one gentle note is there for the secret listener." As he had told Clara that the first movement was a deep lament for her, she probably was the "secret listener" who could detect the "one gentle note."

In the history of recording, there has been but one satisfactory performance of this gigantic piece. That was the pre-war Victor album played by Backhaus. It has never been transferred to LP. The work is extremely hard to play. Its loose-knit organization demands an artist who can make a logical unit of the writing, and there are not many of those around. Technically the writing is extremely demanding, and the coda of the second movement has kept pianists in anguish ever since it was composed. In the concert hall, nobody manages to get through it without a few slips. And the musical problems are just as pronounced. The Elysian last movement can, in less than loving hands, sound repetitious. Unfortunately, none of the current LP versions does full justice to the music. The best is probably Curzon's. The British pianist is careful rather than fiery, especially in the hazardous second movement. He is a genuine artist, but one wishes for a quality of temperament and technical daring commensurate with the nature of the writing. For this is passionate music, and Curzon's playing lacks passion. A pianist who has a superb insight into the music is Perlemuter, and his last movement is, I think, the most beautiful statement of the notes on LP. But he is elsewhere handicapped by a limited finger technique that will not always permit him to put his ideas into effect. Boukoff sounds like a strong pianist—and an inflexible one. Strength rather than poetry marks his interpretation: a Teutonic approach with most of its defects and few of its virtues. Casadesus plays the notes brilliantly enough, failing in the meantime to make much of an emotional experience of the music. It is all very flashy, as he conceives it, and altogether lacking in grandeur. Nor do Demus and Foldes penetrate much below the periphery of the music, while Pennario storms through it in percussive fashion.

——Clifford Curzon. LONDON LL 1009 (with *Kinderscenen, Op. 15*)

——Vlado Perlemuter. Vox PL 9190 (with *Kreisleriana, Op. 16*)

——Yuri Boukoff. EPIC LC 3094 (with *Études symphoniques, Op. 13*)

——Robert Casadesus. COLUMBIA ML 5146 (with *Carnaval, Op. 9*)

——Andor Foldes. DECCA DL 9708 (with

Brahms: *Variations on an Original Theme, Op. 21, No. 1*)

——Joerg Demus. WESTMINSTER XWN 18492 (with *Fantasiestücke, Op. 12*) NOTE: Originally released as WL 5157.

——Leonard Pennario. CAPITOL P 8397 (with Franck: *Prelude, Chorale and Fugue*)

FANTASIESTÜCKE, OP. 12
(*Composed in 1837*)

One of Schumann's most popular collections, the *Fantasiestücke* is made up of a group of short pieces: *Des Abends, Aufschwung, Warum?, Grillen, In der Nacht, Fabel, Traumeswirren,* and *Ende vom Lied.* Now that the Rubinstein disc has been discontinued (RCA VICTOR LM 1072), the best choice is Novaes. Like Rubinstein, she has tone and a singing line. She never fights the piano, and she is an incredible colorist. Unlike many of the younger pianists, she is not afraid to bring out an inner voice: and how this adds to the harmonic and melodic texture! Schumann is full of inner voices, many of them carefully marked in the music—and most pianists blithely ignore them. It is fortunate that we have the distinguished Novaes interpretation, for those of Engel and Demus are pedestrian. Richter's version is not complete. For some reason he plays only six of the eight *Fantasiestücke*, omitting

Grillen and *Fabel*. There is much fine playing here, though one does not hear the peak of perfection as in the Waldscenen (on the reverse of the disc). To my taste, Richter overplays the last section of *Warum?*, drawing it out too fine and making too much of the simple melody. A few blurred measures in *Traumeswirren* remind us that this phenomenal virtuoso is human. He takes a tempo that not even Barere, who used to make a specialty of the piece, ever attempted. No fingers could get through entirely unscathed at this pace.

——Guiomar Novaes. Vox PL 10170 (with *Études symphoniques, Op. 13*)

——Karl Engel. EPIC LC 3070 (with *Faschingsschwank aus Wien, Op. 26*)

——Joerg Demus. WESTMINSTER XWN 18492 (with *Fantasia in C, Op. 17*) NOTE: Originally released as WL 5157.

——Sviatoslav Richter. DECCA DL 9921 (with *Waldscenen, Op. 82; March, Op. 76, No. 2*)

FASCHINGSSCHWANK AUS WIEN, OP. 26
(*Composed in 1839*)

The meaning of this outstanding collection of sibilants is "Carnival Pranks in Vienna." Like much of Schumann's piano music, it is a loose-knit collection of moods sparked by an ardent romanticism. It is in five movements, and each

movement has a diversity of elements. None of
the LP interpretations will provide you with an
unforgettable musical experience. The best of the
three is that of Demus. In this work he offers one
of his best interpretations on discs, playing in a
forceful, well-regulated, tasteful manner. What
he lacks is poetry and flashes of insight. The
recorded sound is much better than on the Blancard disc, which has an unpleasant ping in the
upper register. Blancard is a sensitive pianist,
making more of the lovely intermezzo movement than Demus does, but on the whole the
latter brings the music into sharper relief. Engel
is too matter-of-fact for my taste, and he frequently is much too ponderous.

——Joerg Demus. WESTMINSTER XWN 18061
(with *Arabesque, Op. 18; Blumenstück, Op. 14;
Abegg Variations, Op. 1*)

——Jacqueline Blancard. VANGUARD VRS 416
(with Brahms: *Variations on a Theme by Schumann, Op. 9*)

——Karl Engel. EPIC LC 3070 (with *Fantasiestücke, Op. 12*)

HUMORESQUE, OP. 20
(*Composed in 1839*)

Not played as often as it deserves to be, the
Humoresque is a typical Schumannesque collection of varied ideas assembled into something like

a continuous suite. Schumann referred jokingly
to it as "twelve sheets composed in a week," and
there may even have been twelve sheets if his
script was small. The work as Richter plays it,
with no cuts and all the repeats, runs to about
a half hour (28'20'', to be exact). Richter's performance is one of the great examples of Schumann playing on records. He has imagination,
style and poetry, and fully encompasses the
drama and capriciousness of the music. And what
technical control! The man is a complete master
of the notes, free to concentrate on anything his
brain and fingers desire. He brings out inner
voices, but not excessively so, or in a vulgar
fashion; his dynamics, from triple pianissimo to
fortissimo, are electrifying; his tone remains perpetually singing. All of this comes through recording that is far from perfect. A waver is
present at the opening, and nowhere does the
disc have the tonal clarity one would like to hear.
It makes no difference. Next to this order of
playing, Demus, who seems unmoved by the
engaging melodies under his fingers, fades into
insignificance.

——Sviatoslav Richter. Monitor MC 2022 (with
Franck: *Prelude, Chorale and Fugue*)

——Joerg Demus. Westminster XWN 18496
(with Sonata for *Piano No. 2, in G minor, Op.
22*)   Note: Originally released as WL 5264.

IMPROMPTUS ON A THEME
BY CLARA WIECK, OP. 5
(*Composed in 1833*)

The only LP version ever made in America has
been discontinued, but is mentioned here for the
sake of completeness. Schumann's Op. 5 is a
seldom-played work, and in this case pianists
have good reason for avoiding it. Some fine ideas
are present, but also much padding, and the work
does not hold together very well. Foldes plays
it competently and coldly.

——Andor Foldes. MERCURY 10122 (with *Abegg
Variations, Op. 1; Papillons, Op. 2; Toccata, Op.
7*)

INTERMEZZI, OP. 4
(*Composed in 1832*)

Another discontinued disc, but this one is worth
making an effort to search out. Ever since it was
released, in the middle of 1953, I have been listening to it with admiration. The Intermezzi almost never turns up in concert—Johannesen is
the only pianist within memory to program it—
and yet the music ranks with the *Carnaval* and
Kreisleriana. It has unflagging invention, some of
Schumann's most penetrating melodies, and a
maturity of conception and workmanship that
the composer seldom improved upon. It impresses me as one of Schumann's most personal

pieces, and also one of his most daring. That it is played so seldom is nothing short of a disgrace, and is a sad commentary on the run of concert pianists who learn a given repertoire when students and never develop the intellectual urge to get out of the rut. Johannesen's neat and accurate playing serves the music well. His temperament is not especially romantic, but he has the ability to see the music as an emotional unit, and there is a sense of continuity in his performance. That, plus taste and musicianship, make his performance first-rate.

——Grant Johannesen. CONCERT HALL CHS 1173 (with *Sonata for Piano No. 2, in G minor, Op. 22*)

KINDERSCENEN, OP. 15
(*Composed in 1838*)

Schumann composed several sets of music for children, of which this is by far the most popular (and also the one that contains the *Träumerei*). Later on, the composer was to say that the pieces were not meant *for* children but were a grown-up's memory of childhood, aimed at adults. In addition to *Träumerei*, Op. 15 contains twelve pieces, most of them extremely simple technically, though difficult musically. Despite Schumann's afterthought, young people have been assigned selections from the set immediately after coming out of Czerny. It rejoices in several fine

recorded performances. Zecchi's is very interesting. He strikes a fine balance between intel-
lectualism and emotionalism, does not play down,
and molds his phrases with musicianship. He also
adds many subtleties by bringing out inner
voices, or accenting certain notes in the bass line,
or pedaling with a distinctive style. His tempos
have a spacious quality. In one of the pieces, *Am
Camin*, he does something with the rolled chord
that I have never heard from any other pianist;
it is an imaginative and piquant effect. The interpretation of Novaes is altogether different.
She sounds entirely improvisatory, and she gets
more poetry from the music than any pianist on
LP. Her performance was originally released as
Vox 6900 in May, 1951 (with the *Papillons*) but
was transferred to its present number (with the
Piano Concerto in A minor) in September, 1954.
Horowitz, in his disc, plays simply and tastefully.
He avoids outsized dynamics, and his beautifully
regulated pianism is a delight to hear. Horowitz
has always been especially happy in miniatures
of this kind. Can it be that this thunderer, the
pianist with possibly the biggest command of
sonority in the history of music, is essentially a
miniaturist?

Other excellent interpretations are those of
Gieseking, Curzon and Blancard, though they
strike this listener as just a shade under the three

mentioned above. Gieseking plays with extraordinary fluidity and nuance of tone, but without any special feeling of rapture. He could make the C major scale sound beautiful. One, however, wants a little more. Badura-Skoda plays well, but he does not shape a phrase with the authority of his older colleagues. His is sensitive playing, however, and thoroughly reliable. So is the Haskil performance. The Friedberg disc suffers from blasting recorded sound and playing that is rough despite its command of style.

——Guiomar Novaes. Vox PL 8540 (with *Concerto for Piano and Orchestra, in A minor, Op. 54*) Note: The *Kinderscenen* were originally released on PL 6900.

——Vladimir Horowitz. RCA Victor LVT 1032 (with Chopin: 7 *Mazurkas*) Note: The *Kinderscenen* were originally released on LM 1109

——Carlo Zecchi. Westminster XWN 18139 (with encore pieces)

——Clifford Curzon. London LL 1009 (with *Fantasia in C, Op. 17*)

——Walter Gieseking. Columbia ML 4540 (with Brahms: *Intermezzi, Op. 117*)

——Jacqueline Blancard. Vanguard VRS 415 (with *Sonata for Piano No. 2, in G minor, Op. 22*)

——Paul Badura-Skoda. Westminster XWN

18138 (with *Études symphoniques, Op. 13*)

——Clara Haskil. Epic LC 3358 (with *Wald-scenen, Op. 82*)

——Carl Friedberg. Zodiac 1001 (with *Novel-ette;* Brahms: piano pieces)

KREISLERIANA, OP. 16
(Composed in 1838)

E. T. A. Hoffmann was one of Schumann's inspirations. He was the German ultra-romanticist who was a writer of fantastic tales, a composer and a man of altogether weird imagination. When Schumann composed the *Kreisleriana* (based on the adventures of Johann Kreisler, a character in a Hoffmann volume named *Fantasy Pieces in the Style of Callot*) the author was unknown outside of Germany, and Schumann remarked that the music would be understood only by Germans. (But the dedication is "To my friend, Frédéric Chopin.") As in the case of the Fantasia in C, the best recording of the work has never found its way to LP. I refer to the pre-war Victor album played by Alfred Cortot. But fortunately there· is one satisfactory job. Kempff does magnificently in holding the sometimes rambling work together. His is a mature, cultivated reading. He does not try to overpower the piece, he has a wide tonal palette, and he has sympathy for the idiom. Perlemuter's is a sensitive performance, and had his finger technique been equal to the occasion it would have been outstanding. Unfortunately Perlemuter has to fight the notes. But the French pianist has stylistic authority and manages to communicate much of the music's poetry. The Demus performance is prissy, and Anda's is immature, with pretentious build-ups and interminable ritards.

——Wilhelm Kempff. DECCA DL 9948 (with *Études symphoniques, Op. 13*)

——Vlado Perlemuter. Vox PL 9190 (with *Fantasia in C, Op. 17*)

——Joerg Demus. WESTMINSTER XWN 18489 (with *Romance in F-sharp, Op. 28, No. 2; Toccata, Op. 7*)   NOTE: Originally released as WL 5142.

——Geza Anda. ANGEL 35247 (with *Carnaval, Op. 9*)

NOVELETTES, OP. 21
(*Composed in 1838*)

Blancard is the only pianist ever to have recorded the eight *Novelettes*. Her disc, however, is now discontinued here and is mentioned for the sake of completeness. She plays the music in a sensitive, light-fingered manner. Such honest and musicianly performances are worth respect. Nobody, incidentally, ever programs the *Novelettes* as a unit, nor should they so be played. Each section is a separate work. Nos. 2 and 8 have achieved some concert-hall popularity; the others are not often heard. In WESTMINSTER XWN 18723, Joerg Demus plays the first *Novelette*.

——Jacqueline Blancard. LONDON LL 1266

PAPILLONS, OP. 2
(*Composed in 1832*)

Not as technically difficult as most of the Schumann piano pieces, the tiny *Papillons* (there are eight of them) flicker and vanish. They form a lovely, delicate set, one of the most poetic products of the young Schumann. Novaes has taken care of the work in her inimitable manner. Many of us think it is her finest interpretation on records. It has style, color and flexibility. The delicacy of her fingerwork, the subtlety of her rhythm, the imagination that she lavishes on detail—all these are the work of a great pianist at the height of her powers. Demus plays steadily, and it is his misfortune to have to compete against a transcendent interpretation like the Novaes. A discontinued disc by Kempff (LONDON LL 515) is worth making an effort to locate; it contains a clear, beautifully organized performance of the *Papillons*. K. U. Schnabel on Urania is labored, heavy and explosive.

——Guiomar Novaes. Vox PL 7830 (with *Carnaval, Op. 9*) NOTE: The *Papillons* were originally released on PL 6900, with the Schumann *Kinderscenen, Op. 15*.

——Joerg Demus. WESTMINSTER XWN 18491 (with *Davidsbündlertänze, Op. 6*) NOTE: Originally released as WL 5232.

——Karl Ulrich Schnabel. URANIA 8001 (with Chopin: *Scherzo No. 3, in C-sharp* minor, Op. 39; Liszt: *4 Années de Pélerinage*)

ROMANCES, OP. 28
(*Composed in 1839*)

Three Romances make up Op. 28. Only No. 2, in F-sharp, is popular. It has been recorded by Graffman (VICTOR LM 2190) and Demus (WESTMINSTER XWN 18489). Graffman is stronger and more precise. Pressler is the only pianist to have recorded the entire set. His playing is well regulated, and he has a feeling for the romanticism of the music. A strong clang in the disc interferes with otherwise brilliant recorded sound.

——Menahem Pressler. M-G-M E 3029 (with *Blumenstück, Op. 14*; Mendelssohn: *Variations sérieuses; Rondo Capriccioso*)

SKETCHES FOR PEDAL PIANO, OP. 58
(*Composed in 1845*)

This disc is mentioned here for sake of completeness. Schumann originally composed six Sketches for the pedal piano, a now obsolete instrument. Organists have adopted the music. According to *Grove's*, there are six Sketches, of which Elsasser

plays four, and also a Canon in B minor about
which I can find no reference. The music is not
particularly interesting. Elsasser's playing sounds
perfectly reliable.

——Richard Elsasser. M-G-M E 3007 (with
Mendelssohn: *Sonata for Organ No. 2, in C
minor, Op. 65*)

SONATA FOR PIANO NO. 1,
IN F-SHARP MINOR, OP. 11
(*Composed between 1833 and 35*)

Schumann's first and third piano sonatas are seldom programmed these days (and the third even
less than the first). They are long, often repetitious (the late Harold Bauer used to recommend
long cuts), and hard to hold together. Yet the
F-sharp minor Sonata has so many beautiful moments that its absence is regrettable (and when
Josef Hofmann used to play it, one was never
conscious of its length). It takes a very strong
musical mind, and a brilliant technician, to make
a convincing experience of the work. Brailowsky
is not successful. He hammers away, with a percussive tone and a severely limited set of dynamics (mezzo-forte and up). Badura-Skoda
comes closer to the intent of the music, though
his conception is a little immature and he entirely
misses the meaning of the *alla burla* episode in
the scherzo (Schumann here is poking fun at bad
composers). Badura-Skoda's performance is the

best available, but a more definitive version is needed.

——Paul Badura-Skoda. WESTMINSTER XWN 18490 (with *Carnaval, Op. 9*) NOTE: Originally released as WL 5105.

——Alexander Brailowsky. RCA VICTOR LM 1918 (with works by Mendelssohn, Weber, Schubert)

SONATA FOR PIANO NO. 2, IN G MINOR, OP. 22 (*Composed between 1833 and 38*)

Schumann worked intermittently on the G minor Sonata for over five years, and it was not until 1838 that he composed a new finale. The music is relatively short, composed with economy, and is a fiery, exciting piece that has made itself a familiar concert-hall visitor. As all commentators have pointed out, the writing has none of the rambling quality that disfigures the two other sonatas. Schumann, like Tchaikovsky, was never happy with sonata form, and had to resort to sometimes outlandish, uncomfortable padding to keep matters moving along. None of this happens in the G minor Sonata, with its succinct statement of themes and to-the-point developments. Graffman's able performance is clearly outlined and impeccably delivered. He finds the music much more in his style than the *Études symphoniques* on the reverse. Demus is clear too, but he does not have the rhythmic sharpness of

Graffman. Blancard's supple, sensitive playing somehow lacks excitement, though it is a characteristically reliable performance.

——Gary Graffman. RCA VICTOR LM 2190 (with *Études symphoniques; Romance in F-sharp, Op. 28, No. 2*)

——Jacqueline Blancard. VANGUARD VRS 415 (with *Kinderscenen, Op. 15*)

——Joerg Demus. WESTMINSTER XWN 18496 (with *Humoresque, Op. 20*) NOTE: Originally released on WL 5264.

SONATA FOR PIANO NO. 3, IN F MINOR, OP. 14 (*Composed between 1833 and 36; revised in 1853*)

By all odds, this is the weakest of the three Schumann piano sonatas, and only a fanatic like myself would find things to admire in the music. Its original title was *Concert sans Orchestre*. In 1853 Schumann did some rewriting, and put back a scherzo that originally had been deleted. Both current LP versions are good. I prefer the Goldsand performance. It sounds much more pianistic, and it has more grace and color. The serious Wuehrer tends to lumber along, and he is handicapped by a recording that has as thumpy a bass as I have heard in a long time. Goldsand plays the first edition, Wuehrer the revised one. Goldsand takes an eight-measure cut in the scherzo, while the Wuehrer disc is uncut. Occasionally Goldsand tussles with the notes, but on the whole he is in complete command; and while the Wuehrer performance must be treated with respect, Goldsand's is much more likeable.

In his edition, Harold Bauer points out that Schumann told Heinrich Dorn, one of his teachers, that the sonata was inspired by Clara and "contained the evidences of his struggle for her." The third movement is a set of variations on a theme by Clara. It is for the most part a simple, yearning piece of music, easily the most beautiful thing in the entire sonata. Horowitz has made a beautiful recording of this movement on RCA VICTOR LM 1957. He too sees the music as dreamy introspection, and extends this treatment even to the third variation, which is marked *Passionato*. Horowitz plays it with nocturnal simplicity.

——Robert Goldsand. CONCERT HALL CHS 1147 (with Brahms: *Paganini Variations, Op. 35*)
——Friedrich Wuehrer. Vox PL 8860 (with *Davidsbündlertänze, Op. 6*)

TOCCATA, IN C, OP. 7
(*Composed in 1833*)

Along with Chopin's studies in thirds and sixths, Scriabin's Étude in D flat and parts of the Brahms *Paganini* Variations, the Schumann Toccata is

one of the great bravura exercises in double
notes. It is an extraordinarily effective piece, and
is one of the least introspective things Schumann
ever composed. Lhevinne made this work a specialty, and you can hear his brilliant performance on the Camden reissue (now discontinued,
but worth making every conceivable effort to
locate; it contains some very great piano playing). Barere invariably made a virtuoso stunt of
the Toccata, playing it much too fast, and letting
musical values fall where they may. On the
Remington disc he gets through technically unscathed, but the results are more a tribute to
his amazing fingers than to his musical instincts.
Lewenthal offers quite a flashy, but over-percus-
sive performance. Demus lacks tension.

Josef Lhevinne. RCA CAMDEN CAL 265 (with
Chopin: *Polonaise No. 6, in A-flat, Op. 53;
Études: E-flat, Op. 10, No. 11; G sharp minor,
Op. 25, No. 6; and B minor, Op. 25, No. 10;
Preludes: Nos. 17, in A-flat, and 16, in B-flat
minor;* Schumann-Liszt: *Frühlingsnacht;* De-
bussy-Ravel: *Fêtes;* Strauss-Schulz-Evler: *Blue
Danube Waltz*)

——Simon Barere. REMINGTON R 141 (with
pieces by Rachmaninoff, Blumenfeld, Balakireff,
Liszt and Schumann)

——Raymond Lewenthal. WESTMINSTER XWN
18362 (with encore pieces)

——Joerg Demus. WESTMINSTER XWN 18489
(with *Kreisleriana, Op. 16; Romance, in F-sharp, Op. 28, No. 2*)

WALDSCENEN, OP. 82
(*Composed in 1848-49*)

These "Forest Scenes" consist of nine short
sketches that could just as well be named *Kinderscenen* or *Blumenstücke*. (Schumann was in the
habit of naming his pieces *after* he had composed
them.) They are simple and lovely. Only one of
them, *Vogl als Prophet* ("The Prophet Bird"),
has achieved much popularity, however. I don't
see how the *Waldscenen* could be played better
than by Richter. This pianist, who was born in
1915 in Russia, is one of the greatest of his generation, possibly the greatest. A rather personal
type of interpretation features his playing. It is
often a little withdrawn, technically clean cut,
always elegant. But he can generate plenty of
excitement when necessary, whipping up to a
blazing but always controlled climax. As a master
of tonal resource, color and dynamics, few living
pianists can even come near him. His exceptionally fluent technique enables him to carry off
with flip ease passages that almost everybody else
struggles over (the unisons in No. 2 of the
Waldscenen, for example). Throughout he displays poetry, strength and simplicity, with a

formidable ability to make the inner voices sing out. The *Vogl als Prophet* comes out with a haunting, disembodied quality that I have never heard duplicated, either on records or in the concert hall. Haskil simply cannot match this kind of playing, either technically nor in conception. She is a fine artist but not a very imaginative one, and her playing is all prose against Richter's poetry. And Backhaus sounds angular. His big, severe style does not lend itself easily to these mezzotints; and beautifully as Backhaus sets out the formal propositions of the music, one feels a lack of imagination.

——Sviatoslav Richter. DECCA DL 9921 (with *Fantasiestücke, Op. 12; March, Op. 76, No. 2*)

——Wilhelm Backhaus. LONDON LL 1725 (with Schubert: *Moments musicaux, Op. 94*)

——Clara Haskil. EPIC LC 3358 (with *Kinderscenen, Op. 15*)

Vocal Works

DICHTERLIEBE, OP. 48
(*Composed in 1840; sixteen settings of poems by Heine*)

As a youth, Schumann had composed some songs, but his first twenty-three published works were for the solo piano. It was not until 1840, the year of his marriage, that he started concentrating on the *Lied,* and that year saw a miraculous outburst equaled, in quantity and quality, by no one but Schubert. "Oh, Clara!" he wrote his wife. "What bliss to write songs! Too long have I been a stranger to it." In this year came forth the song cycles of Op. 24, 25, 27, 29-31, 39, 40, 42, 43, 45, 48, 49, 53 and 57. Of these, the crowning achievement is the *Dichterliebe (Op. 48),* which can be translated as "Poet's Love." For this cycle he turned to poetry by one of his favorites, Heine. Here Schumann explores all facets of the *Lied,* from the quiet but soaring lyricism of the first in the cycle, *Im wunderschönen Monat Mai,* to the breathless lightness of *Die Rose, die Lilie, die Taube,* the plaintiveness of *Wenn ich in deine Augen seh'*, the pulsating romanticism of *Ich grolle nicht*, the solemn majesty of *Im Rhein, im heiligen Strome*. A short piano prelude opens the cycle, a more extended postlude for the solo instrument closes it. A singer who undertakes the *Dichterliebe* must bring to it not only voice (which goes without saying), but an ardent, personal approach. It is not a woman's cycle, though several have tried it. The text, for one thing, should be exclusively male property; it can be disconcerting to listen to a woman singing of her (female) beloved. And few women have the vocal powers to encompass the grand moments of the cycle. Even Lotte Lehmann, in her recording, fails to be entirely convincing, though she makes quite an emotional experience of the music. Several things, though, conspire against her. The recording is a transfer from 78-rpm discs and is not very clear in sound. Bruno Walter's accompaniments are too far in the distance, and what is heard is overcautious. Nor is Lehmann in the best of voice, and she sometimes forces it into an occasional edginess. Always she is the sympathetic interpreter, and Lehmann collectors will want the discs without question. But other versions are preferable, including a now discontinued LP disc that contains *two* versions of the *Dichterliebe*—Aksel Schiøtz singing it on one side,

Charles Panzéra on the other (RCA Victor LCT
1132). Another discontinued disc worth looking
for is London LL 940, on which Gérard Souzay
is the admirable baritone in a somewhat dry but
intensely musical and intelligent performance. Of
available discs, the best is that of Dietrich
Fischer-Dieskau. Like Souzay, Fischer-Dieskau's
voice is a little on the dry side and lacks sensuous appeal. But the dignity of the singing, the
accurate pitch and vocal resource, are worthy
of admiration. He is handicapped in his accompanist, Joerg Demus, who fails to rise to the lyric
rapture of the music. Fischer-Dieskau does. As
most baritones do, he transposes many of the
songs anywhere from a semitone to a third down.
Munteanu, a Roumanian tenor, sings in the original keys. His disc suffers from surface noise, and
the singing is a little lachrymose. The voice itself is a fine instrument, but it is used without
much volatility or imagination. Here and there
the accompanist, Franz Holetschek, tries to
nudge Munteanu into faster tempos, to no avail.
——Dietrich Fischer-Dieskau, baritone; Joerg
Demus, piano. Decca DL 9930 (with Brahms:
*Sommerabend, Op. 85, No. 1; Mondenschein,
Op. 85, No. 2; Es liebt sich so lieblich, Op. 71,
No. 1; Meerfahrt, Op. 96, No. 4; Es schauen die
Blumen, Op. 96, No. 3; Der Tod, das ist die
kühle Nacht, Op. 96, No. 1*)

——Lotte Lehmann, soprano; Bruno Walter, piano. COLUMBIA ML 4788 (with *Frauenliebe und Leben, Op. 42*)

——Petre Munteanu, tenor; Franz Holetschek, piano. WESTMINSTER XWN 18010 (with *Liederkreis, Op. 24*)

FRAUENLIEBE UND LEBEN, OP. 42
(Composed in 1840; eight settings of poems by Adelbert von Chamisso)

Always a favorite in the concert hall, *Frauenliebe und Leben* ("A Woman's Life and Love") is relatively short and highly intense. The words are sentimental and even a bit embarrassing, with nowhere near the elegance of the music. Seefried is the most convincing exponent of the cycle on records. Her singing has style and sensitivity behind it, and plenty of vocal splendor. Comparisons with Lehmann are inevitable. Lehmann is more intensely feminine and makes a little more of the words. Seefried, though she never neglects the shades of meaning in the text, relies more fully on pure voice. She is a colorist of amazing deftness, and her voice, with its dark hues and solidity, is a perfectly responsive instrument. Often the sound is pure velvet. She also perfectly carries off the desolate, bleak ending. Lehmann, incidentally, never in life sounded as shrill as she does on her recording of this cycle. Her performance is beautiful, but she has to work against inadequate recorded sound and less than exhilarating piano accompaniments. Jurinac brings to the music a voice of considerable amplitude and color, and an easy, unforced vocal production. Her singing is a pleasure to hear, all the more in that her pitch is perfect. But her interpretations raise a question or two. Her concentration on a beautiful sound almost suggests an end in itself. The songs are not too differentiated. *Helft mir, ihr Schwestern* is sung much the same way as *Du Ring an meinem Finger*, and even the rapturous *An meinem Herzen, an meiner Brust* sounds placid. This lack of intensity and inner conviction puts Jurinac's disc a little below the best. She transposes the last song a semitone down. Ferrier is miscast here. Her enormous voice, reminiscent of Flagstad's, is too big and opulent, and Ferrier apparently could not (or did not care to) throttle down. Everything sounds outsized. She sings the entire cycle a semitone down. Höngen transposes a full tone down. Her voice too is of an operatic calibre that tends to be unwieldy, nor is it always in perfect focus. On the whole a routine and even plodding performance.

——Irmgard Seefried, soprano; Erik Werba, piano. Decca DL 9971 (with Mozart: *An Chloe; Das Lied der Trennung; Das Kinderspiel; Die*

*Verschweigung; Abendempfindung; Die kleine
Spinnerin; Als Luise die Briefe; Einsam ging ich
jüngst; Sehnsucht nach dem Frühlinge*)

——Lotte Lehmann, soprano; Bruno Walter,
piano. COLUMBIA ML 4788 (with *Dichterliebe,
Op. 48*)

——Sena Jurinac, contralto; Franz Holetschek,
piano. WESTMINSTER XWN 18493 (with *Liederkreis, Op. 39*)   NOTE: Originally issued as WL
5345.

——Kathleen Ferrier, contralto; John Newmark,
piano. LONDON 5020 (with Brahms: *Vier ernste
Gesänge, Op. 121*)   NOTE: The Schumann was
originally issued as LL 271 and also 10-inch LD
9068.

——Elisabeth Höngen, contralto; Ferdinand Leit-
ner, piano. DECCA DL 9610 (with Loewe: *Bal-
lads*)

LIEDERKREIS, OP. 24
(*Composed in 1840; nine settings of poems by
Heine*)

None of the songs in this set are concert favorites, though much lovely material is present.
The most popular probably is *Mit Myrten und
Rosen*, the ninth of the cycle (*Liederkreis*, by
the way, means simply "song cycle"), and a
sinuous, impetuous piece of music. Souzay, who
transposes down, sings suavely and turns a phrase
with authority. His heavy gulps of air are dis-

tracting: one case where a listener wishes for lower fidelity. Munteanu has plenty of voice— basically a more pleasing one than Souzay—but his singing is a little crude and does not have much temperament. In dramatic songs like No. 6, *Warte, warte, warte, wilde Schiffmann*, Souzay conveys much more urgency. Souzay, too, is more flexible and is not afraid to use rubato when he feels the musical line calls for it.

——Gérard Souzay, baritone; Dalton Baldwin, piano. LONDON LL 1476 (with Wolf: *Mörike Lieder*)

——Petre Munteanu, tenor; Franz Holetschek, piano. WESTMINSTER XWN 18010 (with *Dichterliebe, Op. 48*)

LEIDERKREIS, OP. 39
(*Composed in 1840; twelve settings of poems by Joseph von Eichendorff*)

In this cycle are such familiar songs as *Intermezzo*, *Waldesgespräch* (one of Schumann's most evocative songs), *Mondnacht* (with its hushed nocturnal atmosphere and intense chromaticism: a masterpiece) and the tremulous, rapturous *Frühlingsnacht* (another masterpiece). Two singers have brought to the music the style and understanding the music deserves. Danco's is poised, accurate, beautiful singing. She uses her silvery voice with unfailing taste, her approach is predominantly lyric, her shading sensitive.

Fischer-Dieskau, who transposes down some of the songs, is more dramatic in his approach. Once in a while he goes in for questionable effects, such as croonings and whisperings, but he knows the music and his singing has authority. He is probably closer to the German ideal of the *Liederkreis,* but I prefer Danco's liquid singing. Jurinac has, if anything, an even better voice than Danco. What she does not have is Danco's instinct for the final finish of a phrase. As in her recording of the *Frauenliebe und Leben,* Jurinac concentrates more on voice than on the relationship between text and music, and she simply does not make the emotional experience of the music that Danco does. Sydney's work is promising but immature, and her pitch is not always accurate. Warfield should have thought twice about releasing his disc. He sounds vocally uncomfortable, and his singing is marked with a noticeable waver. Nor does he show any marked insight into Schumann's world.

——Suzanne Danco, soprano; Guido Agosti, piano. LONDON LL 1324 (with Fauré: *La bonne chanson*)   NOTE: The *Liederkreis* was originally issued as 10-inch LS 590.

——Dietrich Fischer-Dieskau, baritone; Gerald Moore, piano. RCA VICTOR LM 6036 (with Schubert: *Die Winterreise*)   NOTE: The *Liederkreis* occupies the last side of this two-disc set.

——Sena Jurinac, contralto; Franz Holetschek,

piano. WESTMINSTER XWN 18493 (with *Frauen-liebe und Leben, Op. 42*) NOTE: Originally released as WL 5345.

——Lorna Sydney, mezzo-soprano; Wilhelm Loibner, piano. VANGUARD VRS 411 (with Brahms: *Songs for Alto, Viola and Piano, Op. 91; Nachtigall, Op. 97, No. 1; Des Liebsten Schwur, Op. 69, No. 4*)

——William Warfield, baritone; Otto Herz, piano. COLUMBIA ML 4860 (with Brahms: *Vier ernste Gesänge, Op. 121*)

MYRTHEN, OP. 25
(*Composed in 1840; twenty-six settings of poems by Rückert, Goethe, Mosen, Heine, Byron and Moore*)

What a collection! Reposing here are such songs as *Widmung, Der Nussbaum* (as beautiful a song as the mind of man has conceived), *Die Lotos-blume, Aus den hebräischen Gesängen* and *Talismane.* The *Hochländers Abschied* might strike a responsive chord in those who know their Burns: *Mein Herz ist im Hochland, mein Herz ist nicht hier. . . .* Which is, in fact, pretty close in texture and vowel sound to "My heart's in the Highlands, my heart is not here." Perhaps the length of the cycle has deterred singers. Although many of the individual songs are permanent concert-hall residents, nobody has ever dared present the entire cycle at one fell swoop. Of course, *Myrthen* is not like the *Dichterliebe* or *Frauenliebe und Leben*, with a story running through the music, and Schumann probably never intended that it be presented as a unit. The only singer to have recorded all twenty-six songs is Munteanu. He is entirely competent, but does not have enough vocal and emotional variety. As a result, the singing ends up being bland. It is a pity that the owner of such a fine voice does not have more imagination.

——Petre Munteanu, tenor; Franz Holetschek, piano. WESTMINSTER XWN 18006

ZWOLF GEDICHTE, OP. 35
(*Composed in 1840; twelve settings of poems by Justinus Kerner*)

Most of the songs in this collection will prove unfamiliar, though concert-goers will remember the exquisite *Erstes Grün*. Another song that sometimes turns up is *Stille Tränen*. But quite a few of the others are Schumann at his least inspired. Fischer-Dieskau gives a superb performance. His is a big but never vulgar outpouring; his combination of head and heart would prevent vulgarity. Few present-day singers have an equivalent feeling for (as Campion said a few hundred years ago) coupling words and notes lovingly together.

——Dietrich Fischer-Dieskau, baritone; Günther Weissenborn, piano. DECCA DL 9935 (with *Freisinn, Op. 25, No. 2; Schneeglöckchen, Op. 79, No. 26; Ständchen, Op. 36, No. 2; Zwei Venetianische Lieder, Op. 25, Nos. 17 and 18; Das Sennen Abschied, Op. 79, No. 2; Talismane, Op. 25, No. 8*)

SONGS (MISCELLANEOUS)

Several singers have included Schumann songs on recital discs, and an even larger number on discontinued discs that shall not be mentioned here. Taking the singers alphabetically, there is Fischer-Dieskau, who is heard, on DECCA DL 9935, in seven songs: *Freisinn, Op. 25, No. 2; Schneeglöckchen, Op. 79, No. 26; Ständchen, Op. 36, No. 2; Zwei Venetianische Lieder, Op. 25, Nos. 17* and *18; Das Sennen Abschied, Op. 79, No. 2;* and *Talismane, Op. 25, No. 8.* As the other side of the disc is devoted to the seldom-heard *Zwolf Gedichte* of Op. 35, the disc is a major Schumann recital. It is very much worth having. The baritone is in fine, authoritative voice, and he is an artist of consequence. Kirsten Flagstad, on LONDON LL 1546, is vocally amazing. There is so little really great singing today that we are apt to forget, when we come to a wonder like Flagstad, that many great singers of the past continued to give recitals and to be recorded well into old age. A singer with a good vocal method can keep on going indefinitely. That Flagstad has a good vocal method will come as no surprise to anybody. But that she still commands the sheer vocal opulence and security evident on this disc is something that cannot be explained, vocal method or no. She sings all of the songs (*Der Nussbaum, Op. 25, No. 3; Die Soldatenbraut, Op. 64, No. 1; Meine Rose, Op. 90, No. 2; Liebeslied, Op. 51, No. 5; Die Lotosblume, Op. 25, No. 7; Widmung, Op. 25, No. 1; Erstes Grün, Op. 35, No. 4*, and *Im der Fremde, Op. 39, No. 1*) in their original key, she does not skimp, and she produces phrases with the sheen and finish of a singer much younger. As a *Lieder* singer she offers here very much the same kind of interpretation she has offered many times in the past. Her big voice does not sound very intimate and she never has been the most imaginative of recitalists. Indeed, she sings with very little nuance, relying largely on her vocal glory to convey the meaning of a song. In massive pieces she is fine; in a tender, fragile effusion like *Der Nussbaum* she has less luck. There are severe limitations to Flagstad's work as a lieder singer. But for this kind of vocal outpouring we can all be grateful. Edwin McArthur is the accompanist, and the other side of the disc is devoted to five Schubert songs.

Herta Glaz, accompanied by Leo Mueller (M-G-M E 3055) sings eight Schubert songs and nine by Schumann. The Schumann are *Im Wald, Op. 107, No. 5; Die Spinnerin, Op. 107, No. 4; Die letzen Blumen starben, Op. 104, No. 6; Die Soldatenbraut, Op. 64, No. 1; Erstes Grün, Op. 35, No. 4; Ziguenerliedchen, Op. 79, No. 7; Ich wand're nicht, Op. 51, No. 3, Aufträge, Op. 77, No. 5,* and *Melancholie, Op. 71, No. 6.* This is an unusual collection, sung with taste and refinement. If Glaz were a little less detached—she never gets too involved with her material—the disc would be outstanding. As it is, this fine mezzo contributes one of the better Schumann discs in the catalogue. Zinka Milanov, in a recital disc (RCA VICTOR LM 1915) sings *Mondnacht* and *Widmung,* but she is miscast and not even in very good voice. Elisabeth Schwarzkopf also has a recital disc (ANGEL 35023) in which, accompanied by Gerald Moore, she sings two Schumann songs—*Der Nussbaum* and *Aufträge.* She does not convince. For some reason she refuses to allow *Der Nussbaum* to flow naturally, and she overloads it with confidential whispers and other artificial-sounding devices. The great Heinrich Schlusnus, in DECCA DL 9624, can be heard in three Schumann lieder. Accompanied by Otto Braun, he sings *Talismane;* by Franz Rupp, *Die beiden Grenadiere* and *Romanze.*

Schlusnus recorded these on 78-rpm discs and Decca has transferred them to LP. Schlusnus was a baritone who handled himself like John McCormack—with the most exquisite polish, the sweetest of voices and a legato line that starts here and ends there. Unfortunately this is the only Schumann he sings in his five Decca reissues.

Melodrama

MANFRED, OP. 115
(*Composed in 1848-49*)

Three poets above all captured the imagination of the romantic composers—Shakespeare, Byron and Goethe; and of the three it was Byron who most inflamed them. Byron: rich, handsome, titled, romantically handicapped (the club foot), aristocratic scorner of convention and mocker of society, a lady-killer—and a genius too. Small wonder that the artistic young men of Europe adopted Byronic poses, set him to music and tried all they could to identify themselves with him, even to the point of clothing themselves in Byronic dress and turning an affected profile to the world.

Although Byron's *Manfred*, written in Venice in 1817 (at a period when he was arousing even the Venetians with his loose life; and the Venetians do not easily arouse), has three acts and many scene changes, it was obviously never meant for the stage, and Byron was careful to call it a "dramatic poem." In idea and treatment it is strongly suggestive of Marlowe's *Doctor Faustus* (which Byron claimed he had never read) and of Goethe's *Faust* (which Byron had read to him in an oral translation by his friend Monk Lewis). Reviewing *Manfred* in 1820, Goethe wrote: ". . . a wonderful phenomenon, and one that closely touched me. This singularly intellectual poet has taken my *Faustus* to himself and extracted from it the strangest nourishment for his hypochondriac humor. He has made use of impelling principles in his own way, for his own purposes, so that no one of them remains the same; and it is particularly on this account that I cannot enough admire his genius." Goethe complains a little about the "gloomy heat of an unbounded and exuberant despair"; yet he concludes that "the disaffection we feel is always connected with esteem and admiration."

As the poem opens, Manfred bids spirits to arise and obey his bidding. He seeks forgetfulness, but they cannot help him. He hears a voice in an incantation: "I call upon thee! and compel/ Thyself to be thy proper Hell! . . . Nor to slumber, nor to die,/Shall be in thy destiny." (This motivating thought runs throughout the poem.) He attempts suicide on the Jungfrau but is saved by a chamois hunter. He summons the Witch of the Alps, but she can give him no comfort. He invades the regions of Arimanes and has him summon up Astarte (who represents Byron's half-sister and the object of a probably incestuous passion). The poetry here is incandescent: "And I would hear yet once more before I perish/The voice which was my music —Speak to me!/For I have call'd on thee in the still night,/Startled the slumbering birds from the hush'd boughs/ . . . I have outwatch'd the stars,/And gazed o'er heaven in vain in search of thee. . . ." Manfred now awaits his death. He spurns the efforts of the Abbot, who wants to give him spiritual aid, and he dies damned.

The point of the poem is the identification of Byron with Manfred: his wandering, his incapacity for spiritual or emotional release, his conclusion that "knowledge is not happiness, and science/But an exchange of ignorance for that/Which is another kind of ignorance." Manfred cannot rest, knows not what he asks for nor what he seeks. He is the intellectual rebel set apart from humanity.

By modern standards there is a certain amount of posturing and strutting, and a good deal of Gothic nonsense too; but the poem remains a white-hot, tortured cry containing some of the greatest lines that the nineteenth century conceived. And in Scene 4 of the last act, Manfred's final soliloquy comes close to Shakespeare in depth of emotion and purity of language.

Schumann idolized Byron. He had read *Manfred* in 1829 and made a note in his diary to that effect: "*Manfred von Byron—schrechlich!*" In 1848 he composed incidental music for the poem.

He told a friend that he had never devoted himself to any composition with such lavish "love and power."

He did not use the entire poem. For his score he composed an overture (the only section commonly played today), four musical sections to Act I, seven to Act II, and four to Act III. Much of this is "melodrama"—that is, musical background against a recitation (the role of Manfred is a speaking, not a singing part). The melodrama was a form taken quite seriously in the early eighteenth century. The grave-digging episode in Beethoven's *Fidelio* is a melodrama. Schubert and Berlioz composed some, and one can find the form as late as Richard Strauss' *Enoch Arden*. Getting back to *Manfred:* Schumann also composed several choruses, several vocal solos and an orchestral entr'acte that prefaces Act II.

All of the music is present in this recording, though Beecham has made a few additional cuts in the poem, shifted some sections around, and added some poetry not included by Schumann, including the great tower soliloquy.

On first hearing, the music may appear minimal. Certain things immediately stand out— "When the moon is on the wane," with its use of the main theme from the *Études symphoniques;* the exquisite entr'acte; the songs of the spirits. But on the whole, one's attention is riveted on the rolling, sonorous voice of George

Rylands, who reads the verse with full respect not only for its meaning but also for its own musical values, divorced from Schumann's contribution. Rylands' delivery has been accused of being old-fashioned, but I cannot think of any better way for the lines to be read.

As one replays the discs, the composer's commentary takes on more and more value. Naturally the music is episodic and undeveloped, but I know nothing in the entire body of Schumann's orchestral music to surpass the poignancy and piercing yearning of the background to Manfred's apostrophe to Astarte. A positively other-worldly quality is communicated. Only in several sections does the inspiration fall off: the conventional Latin hymn at the end, and the chorus of demons (what Berlioz would have done here!). Otherwise this is Schumann at his most imaginative and most delicate. There is not too much of it, for a good section of *Manfred* remains declamation, but what there is remains unforgettable.

The recording is beautiful. Beecham, with his usual taste, does not try to push the orchestra into prominence during the melodramas, contenting himself with quietly reinforcing the mood. (Even the engineers have cooperated; the volume at the end of the Astarte sequence drops to such a pianissimo that the music is actually difficult to hear.) In the well-known overture,

Beecham leads a stirring, romantic performance without ever becoming mannered, and he is fortunate in his flexible chorus and his competent cast of singers and actors. There is only one tiny fluff. Some editions of the poem contain a misprint in Act III, when the Abbot refers to the "sacred peasantry." Byron wrote "scared peasantry." Laidman Browne, reading the line, says something like this: "My pious brethren— the sacr—*scared* peasantry." This little hitch might have been edited out of the tape. One other mild complaint: the liner notes are interesting and informative as far as they go, but they are woefully inadequate. The year of composition of the poem is not mentioned, nor is a clue given as to when Schumann composed the music. It seems a pity that in a two-disc recording as unusual as this, the annotator was not given enough space to develop the ideas he only broaches.

——Speakers: George Rylands (Manfred); Jill Bacon (Witch of the Alps and Astarte); Raf de Torre (Nemesis and the Spirit Genius of Manfred); Laidman Browne (A Spirit and Abbot of St. Maurice); David Enders (Chamois Hunter and Servant of Manfred). Singers: Gertrude Holt, Claire Duchesneau, Niven Miller, Glyndwr Davies, Ian Billington. BBC Chorus, Royal Philharmonic Orchestra, Sir Thomas Beecham, cond. Columbia M2L 245, two discs.